Understanding People in Society

CW01430219

The World & You

Deakin & Graham
Series Editor: Muir Johnstone

USA, Land of Opportunity?

The Media...

Decisions

Rich/Poor World.?.!

Hodder & Stoughton

ACKNOWLEDGEMENTS

The authors would like to thank the following people for their help in producing this book:
John Bruce (Pupil Profile Grids)
Marion G. Graham (Additional Research)
Janice Govan (Additional Research)
Elizabeth Deakin (Secretarial Support)
Jim McColl (Consultancy)

The publishers would like to thank the following for permission to reproduce copyright photographs in this volume:

J. Allan Cash Ltd pp16 (*not* parks, schools, social work), 17 (social security); Anheuser-Busch p87 (Sea World); Circa Photo Library/John Smith p45; Crown Copyrights/MoD p18 (defence); Flying Colours Photography Ltd p22 (left); Liberal Democrats p22; NASA's Kennedy Space Center p88; Graham Piggott p22 (Hague); Robert Harding Picture Library pp4, 8, 16 (social work), 17 (NHS), 69 (right); RHPL © Tom Ang p16 (parks); RHPL © Alain Eurard p71; RHPL © Nigel Francis pp84 (Capitol), 89; RHPL © T. Gervis p94; RHPL © J. Lightfoot p87 (MGM); RHPL © J. Miller p17 (Parliament); RHPL © Julian Pottage p17 (Job Centre); RHPL © W. Rawlings pp18 (trade), 121; SNP p22; Topham Picturepoint pp16 (top), 49, 51, 72, 73, 74, 76, 84 (2), 102, 103; Topham Picturepoint © Lee Snider p100; Associated Press/Topham Picturepoint © A. Nadel p105; Press Association/Topham p18 (foreign affairs); Tony Stone Worldwide (Beryl Bidwell) p16 (schools); Tony Stone Images (Stewart Cohen) p69 (left); Tony Stone Images (Mark Douet) p18 (prisons); Tony Stone Images (Andy Sacks) p18 (industry); Tony Stone Images (Bob Torrez) p91; Universal Studios Florida, © 1998 UCSI p88. The article reproduced on p6 is from the *Sunday Post*.

Every effort has been made to trace and acknowledge copyright. The publishers will be glad to make suitable arrangements with any copyright holders whom it has not been possible to contact.

Cartoons by Richard Duszczak
Illustrations by Peter Bull
Maps and diagrams by Jean-Charles Chamois

Orders: please contact Bookpoint Ltd, 39 Milton Park, Abingdon, Oxon OX14 4TD. Telephone: (44) 01235 400414, Fax: (44) 01235 400454. Lines are open from 9.00–6.00, Monday to Saturday, with a 24 hour message answering service. Email address: orders@bookpoint.co.uk

British Library Cataloguing in Publication Data
A catalogue record for this title is available from The British Library

ISBN 0 340 70149 8

First published 1998

Impression number	10	9	8	7	6	5	4	3	2	1
Year				2002	2001	2000	1999	1998		

Typeset by Wearset, Boldon, Tyne and Wear.
Printed in Great Britain for Hodder & Stoughton Educational, a division of Hodder Headline Plc, 338 Euston Road, London NW1 3BH by Scotprint Ltd, Musselburgh, Scotland.

CONTENTS

Preface

For the teacher

The central aim of this book and its companion text is to provide a comprehensive and adaptable programme of study for the Environmental Studies 5–14 Attainment Outcome Understanding People in Society.

The series is comprehensive in that it covers all relevant Key Features and Strands as defined in the Environmental Studies 5–14 National Guidelines published by the Scottish Office Education and Industry Department. Since the books and their accompanying support packages provide altogether 14 self-contained study units for Understanding People in Society, there is ample scope for teachers to select and permutate units into adaptable and varied programmes of study. There are seven primary topics covering P4 to P7, with suggestions for teaching People in Society in the infant stages. The first chapter in the secondary textbook is conceived as a bridging unit incorporating P7 and S1 study programmes. The other six study units provide a balanced and progressive course of study for the S1/S2 stage.

The support materials are designed to help teachers and pupils make the best use of the study package. Each chapter presented in the companion books has an accompanying section of support materials: detailed syllabus plans set out clearly the People in Society Key Features and Strands covered in each unit, and offer guidance on teaching approaches and appropriate learning activities for pupils using the textbooks. Individual learning tasks are identified for specific Attainment Targets (at Levels A to F).

The materials provide photocopiable helpsheets and tasksheets for use by pupils studying the units covered in the textbooks. Examples of pupil attainment records/profiles are also provided.

For pupils

You will see the following symbols throughout your textbook. Each symbol tells you something.

❶ Note   You will need a pencil and paper, as you will be writing.

❷ Research   You have to investigate or study something carefully.

❸ Discuss   Here you will discuss ideas with a partner, with a group or as a class.

❹ Question   Think carefully before you answer.

Rules
– Who Needs Them?

1

Once Upon a Time – A Story to Begin With!

A long time ago, a man called Daniel Defoe wrote a story about someone called Robinson Crusoe, who was shipwrecked alone on a desert island. Perhaps you have heard the story or read the book or even seen it as a cartoon on television.

Robinson Crusoe had many exciting adventures on the island, but he also spent a lot of his time working. He had to do everything for himself, because there was no-one there to help him. He had to make himself safe and comfortable on the island by building a shelter, looking for food and making clothes. After a while he became very lonely. He missed human company – someone to talk to, to share his work and to explore the island with. However, he also knew that because he was alone on the island, he could do exactly as he wanted. There was no-one to tell him what to do. No-one to threaten him. No-one to bully him. He was able to do exactly what he wanted to do, when he liked, and everything on the island belonged to him. There were no rules for him to have to follow and because there were no rules, there were no punishments for breaking rules. Later in the story, after Crusoe had been on the island for a few years, he rescued someone who had been brought to the island by cannibals to be eaten. Crusoe called his new friend Friday, after the day when he had saved him. Now, for the first time in the story, Crusoe was not alone on the island, and because there were now two people sharing the island, rules had to be made, and there had to be punishments along with the rules. Crusoe made three important rules which Friday had to obey:

★ Friday had been a cannibal and Crusoe made him promise never to eat any humans again;

★ Crusoe's shelter was his own and Friday must never come into it;

★ Friday was not allowed to touch any of Crusoe's weapons.

The punishment which went with all three rules, was that if Friday broke any of them, Robinson Crusoe would kill him.

In this story we can see how rules and punishments have to be made when people live and share with each other. Rules and punishments are one way of trying to make sure that people behave properly towards each other, whether on a desert island, or in a family, or in a school, or in a community.

The story of Robinson Crusoe and Friday had a happy ending. They learned to trust each other and became great friends – but we won't spoil it for you because you may want to read it for yourself.

ACTIVITY ONE

Draw a box like the one below. Fill in at least FIVE good things and FIVE bad things for Robinson Crusoe, living alone on the island (before he met Friday). The first one has been done to help you. Some are in the story, but try to imagine yourself alone on a desert island and think of other things:

Good things (advantages)	Bad things (disadvantages)
No-one to bully him	He might feel lonely

❶ Why do you think Crusoe had to build a shelter for himself on his desert island? Can you think of three reasons?

❷ Why do you think Crusoe chose the three rules he did when Friday came?

❸ What might Crusoe have been afraid of?

❹ What was to be the punishment if Friday broke any of the rules?

Do you think the rules made by Crusoe were fair?

Was the punishment for breaking the rules fair?

Should Friday have been given the chance to say what he thought?

Should Friday have been allowed to make some rules of his own?

Was Crusoe correct in believing that as he was on the island first it belonged to him?

Living in Groups

When people have to live in groups, just like Robinson Crusoe and Friday – when people live together, work together, or play together – there have to be rules which make sure we treat each other fairly. You are a member of lots of groups. Some are easy to think of. You are in a group right now – your class!

ACTIVITY TWO

Draw a box in the centre of your notebook. Draw yourself in the box, and around the box write down the groups you are a member of. You should be able to think of at least five or six.

What – No Rules! Yippee!

Have you ever thought how great it would be if we didn't have any rules? Try to think of ten things you would like to do if there were no rules. Things like, perhaps, not coming to school, or staying up late, or eating all the chocolate biscuits at home! Even better – if there were no rules, there would be no punishments! What punishments do you hate most? Think of the three you would most like to do away with!

ACTIVITY THREE

Choose one of the following:

Home   School   Out playing   Sport   Club/organisation

Write a few sentences saying what you would most like to do in one of these if there were no rules or punishments.

Rules on the Road?

But wait a minute! Perhaps it might not be as great fun as we first thought! Let's look at an example of what might happen if there were no rules for something which affected not only us, but everyone. Let's imagine there were no rules for using the roads. Not only for car drivers, but for all of us who have bikes, skateboards and rollerblades, and also for pedestrians. Right now, everyone has to follow something called the Highway Code, which is a list of rules to make things safe for road users. Let's imagine there was no Highway Code, no rules for using the roads. It might not be great fun now!

ACTIVITY FOUR

Put the heading in your notebook, 'No Rules for the Road'. Try to think of ten examples of dangerous or terrible things which could happen if there were no rules at all for people using the roads – drivers, cyclists, pedestrians. Here is an example to get you started: drivers could drive on any side of the road, or even on the pavement. To help you a little more, here are ten words jumbled up which each have to do with road users. Try to unscramble them.

SILTYCC	RIVERD	SUB
FACTFIR		RORYL
GRAPINK		DESEP
RAIDSTEPNE	GREENPASS	STIGLH

But Nobody Asked Me!

Now perhaps we are beginning to understand why rules and punishments have to be made. Even if we do understand, rules and punishments can still seem very unfair to us, because nobody ever seems to ask us what we think. Do your mum or dad ever ask you what the rules and punishments should be at home? Does your teacher ever ask you what the class rules should be? Does the referee in a sport you play ever ask you what rules you would like for the game? Does any adult ever ask you for your views or opinions on rules?

Perhaps an important reason for us not liking rules is because no-one asks us what rules we would like. It seems that most rules only tell us what not to do, and they often spoil our fun; and, of course, if we do break the rules, we are punished. The same people who make the punishments, make the rules. This often seems unfair. Sometimes we may be punished for breaking a rule we didn't even know existed!

Let's think about some rules and punishments that affect us every day.

ACTIVITY FIVE

Copy this grid into your notebook and try to complete it.

RULES	My family	My class or school	A sport I play/watch	A club or group I'm in
Who makes the rules				
An example of ONE rule				
Punishment for breaking this rule				
Did you help make this rule?				
Were you asked about punishment?				
Should you have a say?				

Rules and Laws for Young People

Perhaps another important reason we do not like rules is that they very often seem to be unfair to children and young people. You know the sort of thing – signs on shop doorways which say 'No school children allowed' or 'Only two school pupils at a time'. This type of rule is very different from laws which affect young people. Laws give minimum ages at which young people are allowed to do certain things. There are different ages for different things, and this can be very confusing. It can be difficult to work out when childhood ends and adulthood begins. For example, you can get married at 16 but cannot vote until you are 18. You can pass your driving test at 17 but cannot watch certain films until you are 18.

ACTIVITY SIX

Look at the table overleaf, which shows you the ages at which you are allowed to do certain things in Scotland, and answer these questions.

❶ What rights do you have as soon as you are born?

❷ When can you be convicted of a criminal offence?

Are you old enough to buy a goldfish?

IN DAYS past, 21 was the age when you were given the key to the door. These days 18 is the age at which you're legally considered an adult.

But don't think you have to wait that long to have rights — you have some from the moment you're born.

Here's a breakdown of some of the rights and entitlements certain birthdays bring you.

Birth — Bank or building society account can be opened in your name; You can own Premium Bonds.

5 — Must receive full-time education.

7 — Draw cash out of your bank, building society or PO account.

10 — Be convicted of a criminal offence.

12 — Buy a pet without your parent being present.

14 — Take on a part-time job; own an airgun; go into a bar with an adult, but not to buy or consume alcohol.

16 — Marry without parents' consent (Scotland only, parents' consent needed in rest of UK); apply for supplementary benefit; choose your own doctor; drive a moped or tractor; buy cigarettes; join the armed forces with parents' consent (male).

17 — Drive a car or motorcycle; enter a betting shop, but not bet; join the armed forces with parents' consent (female).

18 — You can vote; marry without parental consent; change your name; apply for a passport; bet; obtain credit; be eligible for jury service; buy drinks in a pub; donate blood and organs.

21 — Stand in a general or local election; apply for a liquor licence; drive a lorry or bus.

❸ When can you start earning a wage?

❹ What are the differences between males and females on joining the army?

❺ Why do you think 18 is the age at which you are legally considered an adult?

❻ Why do you think there are still some things you can't do until you are 21?

 Do you think it would be more sensible if there was one age for all of these things? Would this cause problems? Do you think most young people are adults at 16?

Now It's Our Turn – Let's Make Some Rules

Rules Are Everywhere

School

Sport

Rules are made to **protect** us.
Rules are made to keep us **safe**.
Rules are made to treat everyone **fairly** and **equally**.
Earlier, we found out that the reason we might not like some rules is because no-one asked us what we thought! Well, now someone is asking us!

ACTIVITY SEVEN

Let's imagine that this is a new class with a new teacher, who is giving you the chance to make up a new set of class rules. In groups of four or five, try to draw up a list of ten rules which your group agrees would be fair and reasonable to have in the class.

Then have a look at the other groups' rules and compare them to your own. With your teacher, see if you can agree on ten rules which the whole class thinks would be fair. Perhaps when you are thinking of rules you should also be thinking about the reasons for them. For example, 'Do not swing on your chair' might be a sensible class rule, because if you did you could tumble over and hurt yourself. If you are really sensible, your teacher may even let you think about what suitable punishments there might be for the rules you draw up!

If everyone agrees to these rules, it might be called the 'Class Contract'. Include your rules in a copy of the contract below.

The Class Contract

Class Contract

We, the pupils and teacher of Class ____ in _____ school, state that the rules below have been made and agreed by us. We think they are fair and easy to understand. We will try to keep to these rules because we think they will help us work better together as a class. If the rules are broken, some punishment may have to be given. We will accept this punishment if it is fair and if we deserve it.

Class Rules

1. _____
2. _____
3. _____
4. _____
5. _____
6. _____
7. _____
8. _____
9. _____
10. _____

Signed _____ Teacher _____ Pupil

Now Let's Be Honest About Rules!

Perhaps we now realise why rules are important. We may not always like them, but at least we now understand why we need them. Think back to earlier in this section when we thought about there being no rules at all.

ACTIVITY EIGHT

Copy the checklist below into your notebook. Try to complete it as honestly as possible, remembering what we have learned so far about rules.

Class Rules Checklist

1) For my class I would like to see (✓)

    _____ Rules   _____ No Rules

2) I would like the rules a lot better if I could help to make them

    _____ Yes   _____ No

Reasons _____

               _____

               _____

3) If there were rules for this class I would

feel safer	_____	work harder	_____
be happier	_____	have less fun	_____
learn more	_____	learn less	_____
behave better	_____	like school less	_____
be bored	_____	be punished	_____

(Tick as many boxes as you like)

4) I think the idea of a Class Contract is

    _____ Good   _____ Bad   _____ Don't Care

5) I think the punishments should be decided by

Teacher _____   Pupils _____   Parents _____   All of us _____

Now Let's Play Teacher

ACTIVITY NINE

Now is your chance to play teacher! Read the details of these crimes below and decide what punishments each should receive. The 'crimes' will probably be very familiar to you!

What punishment would you give to someone in the class who was

a) cheeky to the teacher

b) interrupted others

c) was often late

d) copied neighbour's work

e) told lies to get others into trouble

f) stole from others in the class

g) often forgot to do homework

h) kept swinging on their chair

i) swore at the teacher

j) fell asleep during lessons?

(Try to think of a different punishment for each crime.)

Now list these crimes in order of importance 1–10. Make what you think is the most serious crime number 1 and so on down to number 10, the least serious. Compare your ideas with others in the class. Do most of them agree with what you think is the most serious crime? Ask your teacher to compare his/her list with yours. How good at playing teacher were you?

Why Do We Need Punishments?

Now see if you can work out four important reasons why we need to punish people who break the rules.

ACTIVITY TEN

Use the jumbled-up letters to fill the blank spaces in the four sentences below.

❶ To try to stop the person who breaks the rules from harming other people:
CEPTROT = P _ _ _ _ _ _

❷ To try to help the person who breaks the rules to change for the better:
FROMER = R _ _ _ _ _

❸ To try to stop the person who breaks the rules from doing it again:
TERDE = D _ _ _ _

❹ To get our own back on those who break the rules and make them suffer:
ENGEVER = R _ _ _ _ _ _ _

Must We Always Follow Rules?

Sometimes people can break rules for good reasons, and they may not be punished. Can you think of an example where you might break a rule and not be punished? Let's think back to the story of Robinson Crusoe. Remember the three rules that Crusoe made for Friday? In the story, Friday broke two of these rules because he had a very good reason to do so, and Crusoe did not punish him. Maybe you can work out for yourself which two he broke and what his reason was. If not, you will have to read the story or ask someone to tell you what happened.

What Next?

You have done very well so far in working your way through this section on rules. You may even have enjoyed some of it. You have also learned a lot about why we need rules and why there have to be punishments. You have begun to think about the part you play in groups, whether it is in your family, school or local community.

In secondary school, your Environmental Studies course called 'People in Society' will give you a lot more opportunities to think and talk about the part you play in groups, and this will build upon what you are doing in your primary school. We will learn a lot more about who makes the rules for our community, our country, and for Europe. We will learn a lot more about the part we can play as citizens of Scotland, the UK, Europe and the world. We will compare our lifestyles with those of people in other parts of the world. We will hopefully learn how to be good family members, good pupils and good citizens. We will be looking at topics such as the following:

Environmental Studies – People in Society

Topics We Will Look At

Who Represents Us	Scotland and Europe
The United Nations	Family and Society
Television and Newspapers	Human Rights
The USA	Rich World, Poor World

Activities We Will Complete

Group Work	Running an Election Campaign
Research and Investigations	Role-play
Discussion	Interviews
Graphics and Illustrations	Writing Letters and Visiting Speakers
Visits	Keeping a Logbook/Notebook

Technology We May Use

Computers	CD-ROM
Video Camera	Audio Cassette
Diastar	Overhead Transparency
Television	Slides and Photographs

What We Will Do Next

You will have the chance to listen to others, give your own views, make up your own mind and reach your own conclusions. You will learn how to find out whether someone is being biased or whether they are exaggerating. You will be able to make up your own mind about things.

And Finally!

Sometime soon, when you start your secondary school and you meet your Modern Studies teacher, you will be able to go through your Environmental Studies 'People in Society' course, where you will be given the chance to think about some of the issues that affect our lives.

How are elections run?	What is the third world?	What is the United Nations?
How powerful is advertising?	Can we help the elderly more?	Who makes the rules in our society?
Who are the rich and poor?	**ENVIRONMENTAL STUDIES**	Can we solve inter-national problems?
Are we Scottish, British or European?	**PEOPLE IN SOCIETY**	How can I become a good citizen?
What laws affect young people?	How we have a say in how our society is run	Why do we pay taxes?
What is a superpower?	Can we stop wars?	Do my views matter?

11

2 Decisions – Who Makes Them?

Our New School

In school, there are lots of rules which we have to follow. There are a number of different people in the school, whose job it is to make sure the rules are followed by everyone. The titles of some of these people are listed below:

Deputy Head Teacher   **Head Teacher**

Register Teacher   **Assistant Head Teacher**
                    (Lower School – First and Second Year)

Guidance Teacher

ACTIVITY ONE

1. Can you write down what the main job of each type of teacher is?

2. Beside their titles, fill in the names of the people in these jobs. Your teacher will help you.

3. Write down one school rule you know, which you think is a good rule, and say why it is good.

4. Write down one school rule which you think is a bad one, and say why.

5. List the punishments for breaking the school rules shown below, in order of how serious they are. Number them 1 to 6, starting with the least serious:

Suspension   **Detention**   **Punishment exercise**
Warning   **Expulsion**   **Parents up to school**

Rules in the Community

Just as we have rules in our school to keep things running smoothly, we also have rules in our community. These rules are called **laws**, and we have to follow them whether we like it or not.

Some of the laws apply to everyone in the whole country. They are called **national** laws. For example, there are laws about driving on the left-hand side of the road. If we go abroad on holiday we have to remember that in most places, they drive on the right-hand side of the road.

Other laws only apply to people living in our local area. They are called local **bye-laws**. For example, it may be that in our local area, there are grassy areas where we are not allowed to play any ball games or drink alcohol in public.

ACTIVITY TWO

❶ Can you list another three national laws which apply to everyone?

❷ Can you list another three Local Bye-Laws which apply in your area?

Courts

When we break the rules in our school, we have to suffer the consequences and take our punishment. It is exactly the same in our community, though the punishments can be a bit more severe. It is not likely that we can be locked up for the night if we 'forget' our homework.

The table below shows the three main levels of **courts** which can decide what happens to us if we break the laws.

Courts	Offences	Examples	Examples
District Court	minor offences		
Sheriff Court	more serious offences		
High Court	most serious offences		

ACTIVITY THREE

Copy the table above into your jotters, and see if you can fill in two examples of the types of crime that might be dealt with in each court.

Taking Part in Decision Making

When we arrived in our new school, there were lots of rules which were already in place, that we had to follow. Now that we have been here for a while, we might have our own ideas about these rules. But will anyone listen to us? What can we do to attract attention to the things that bother us, and will anyone do anything about it?

When we are faced with large numbers of people who all want to have a say in making decisions, it seems to be a good idea for someone to act on our behalf, that is, to **represent** us.

Representation, Rights and Responsibilities

We have to make sure we choose the right person to represent us, and that we are allowed to make the choice ourselves. We also have to make sure that although we listen to the views of most of the group who want one thing (they are known as the **majority**), we should also listen to the views of others in the group (known as the **minority**). It is also very important for us to accept a decision once it is made – if it is made fairly – and to be able to say, 'This might not be a decision I like, but it is what the majority want, and I have to go along with it.' This is a **responsibility** we have to accept if we take part in reaching decisions with others. We should not have the **right** to choose a representative if we are not going to accept the decision of the majority.

ACTIVITY FOUR

Two of the most important rights we have in this country are the right to a free education and the right to freedom of speech. Can you think of four other rights we have, and put them into your notebook? Discuss these in groups.

Who Represents Us?

As we have seen already, perhaps the best way for us to take part in making decisions, is to get someone to act on our behalf, that is, to represent us. We saw earlier that it is quite important to make sure that we have a say in choosing our own representatives. However, there are also a number of other rules that we should have when making this choice.

ACTIVITY FIVE

Look at the list of rules shown below and overleaf that we might have for choosing our representatives. Copy each one into your notebook and say whether we should have it or not..Give a reason for your answer. Should there be:

★ a choice of people to vote for (they are called candidates)?

★ a rule on how long they should represent us?

★ any rules on who is allowed to become a candidate?

★ any rules on who is allowed to vote?

★ any rules on how voting should take place (a show of hands)?

Local Councils

In Britain there are different types of elected representatives. There are **local** and **national** representatives. The people elected to represent us at the local level are called **councillors,** as they meet together in the local Council. The people elected to represent us at the national level are called **Members of Parliament (MPs),** as they meet together in **Parliament,** in London. Soon members of the Scottish Parliament (MSPs) will meet together in Edinburgh. We will be looking at MPs and MSPs later, but first of all we will look at our local Council.

Map One – The Map of Scotland – Local Council Areas

	Council Area	Voters	%	Population
1	City of Aberdeen	91,070	53.7	218,220
2	Aberdeenshire	97,036	57.0	223,630
3	Angus	52,149	60.2	111,020
4	Argyll & Bute	45,482	65.0	90,550
5	Clackmannanshire	23,598	66.1	48,660
6	Dumfries & Galloway	73,799	63.4	147,900
7	Dundee	65,211	55.7	153,710
8	East Ayrshire	60,864	64.8	123,820
9	East Dunbartonshire	59,013	72.7	110,220
10	East Lothian	45,228	65.0	85,640
11	East Renfrewshire	45,926	68.2	86,780
12	Edinburgh	217,579	60.1	441,620
13	Falkirk	69,937	63.7	142,610
14	Fife	166,554	60.7	351,200
15	Glasgow	246,284	51.6	632,850
16	Highland	99,982	60.3	206,900
17	Inverclyde	40,890	60.4	89,990
18	Midlothian	39,827	65.1	79,910
19	Moray	37,124	57.8	86,250
20	North Ayrshire	67,562	63.4	139,020
21	North Lanarkshire	149,956	60.8	326,750
22	Orkney	8,328	53.5	19,760
23	Perth & Kinross	65,667	63.1	130,470
24	Renfrewshire	87,400	62.8	176,970
25	Scottish Borders	54,181	64.8	105,300
26	South Ayrshire	60,303	66.7	113,960
27	South Lanarkshire	148,257	63.1	307,100
28	Shetland	8,736	51.5	22,830
29	Stirling	42,797	65.8	81,630
30	West Dunbartonshire	46,347	63.7	97,790
31	West Lothian	71,884	62.6	146,730
32	Western Isles	12,676	55.8	29,410

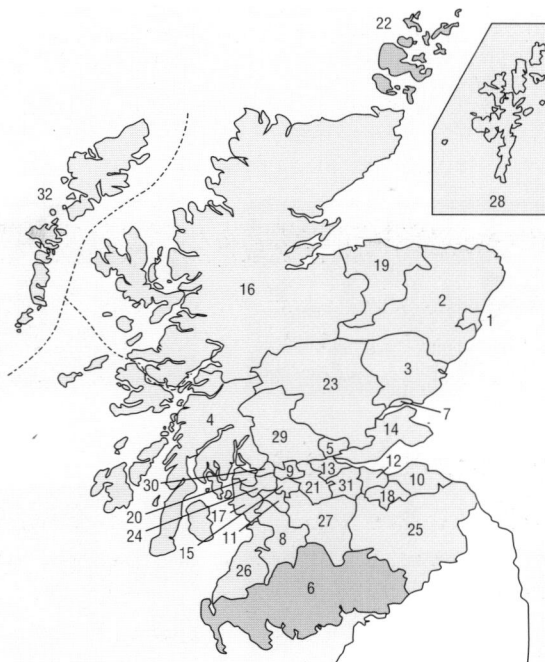

ACTIVITY SIX

❶ What is the Council area you live in called?

❷ What are the main towns in your Council area?

❸ How many Council areas are there altogether in Scotland?

❹ Find out how many councillors there are in your local Council.

❺ Find out the name of the Councillor who represents you

What Do Councils Do?

Local Councils are responsible for providing us with some very important **services** that we could not do without. What you are doing right now – hopefully learning in a class in a school – is one of these services. You will probably be surprised at the number of things Councils do for us, and when you find out what these services are, you will begin to realise how important the local Council is. You should also begin to see what job our councillors are doing for us and why it is important to take part in Council elections.

Town Hall, Oxford

ACTIVITY SEVEN

Below you will see photos of a number of different services which are provided by the local Council. On the following page are some sentences which explain what each of these services is all about. See whether you can match up the services with the sentences, and copy them into your notebook.

HOUSING

TRANSPORT

CLEANSING

POLICE

PARKS

LIBRARIES

COMMUNITY CENTRES

SCHOOLS

SOCIAL WORK

1. A place where people can hold meetings, play games, and join clubs.

2. A service which includes buses and trains and allows people to travel.

3. A service which protects the public and keeps law and order.

4. A place with plenty of fresh air to relax and enjoy yourself.

5. A place for learning about your local community and passing exams.

6. A service to provide people with some shelter and to live in comfort.

7. A service to help people with family problems and other difficulties.

8. A service to keep the community clean and tidy.

9. A place to borrow books and to provide you with other useful information.

The National Government

As we saw earlier, we elect our local Councillor to represent us in the local area. These local Councillors make decisions about the local services they provide for us. Many decisions are not taken at the local level, however, and are taken in London instead. As we live in a **democracy**, we also get the chance to choose a representative to act on our behalf in London. They are called **Members of Parliament** or **MPs** for short, as they go to the **Houses of Parliament** at **Westminster** in London. Parliament makes decisions on matters of national importance. The Scottish Parliament will make decisions on matters to do with Scotland. We will look first at the National Government in Westminster.

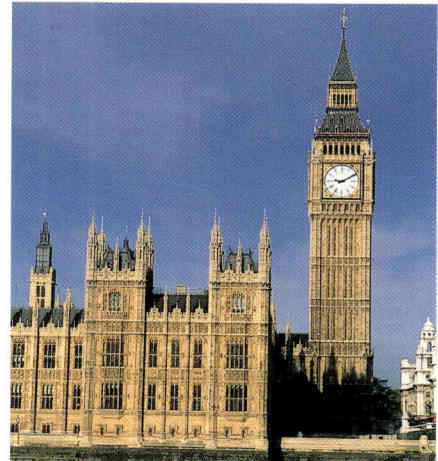

ACTIVITY EIGHT

Below and overleaf you will see some photos showing a number of different services which are provided by the national government. Underneath the photos are some sentences which explain what each of these services is all about. See if you can match up the services with the sentences, and copy them into your notebook.

SOCIAL SECURITY: DSS   NATIONAL HEALTH SERVICE   EMPLOYMENT

PRISONS: WORMWOOD
SCRUBS, LONDON

INDUSTRY

TRADE: STOCK
EXCHANGE, LONDON

FOREIGN AFFAIRS:
FOREIGN SECRETARY
ROBIN COOK IN INDIA

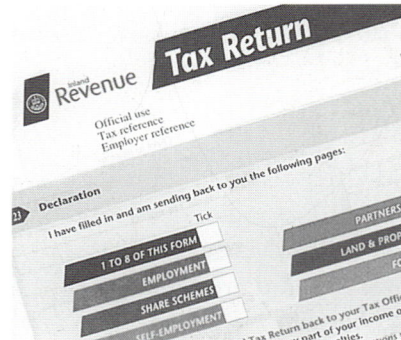

TAXATION

DEFENCE: MINISTRY OF
DEFENCE, LONDON

❶ The Government gives us places to go to look for jobs, and gives training.

❷ The Government deals with other countries and signs agreements.

❸ The Government tells us how much we have to pay for these services.

❹ The Government protects us from dangerous criminals.

❺ The Government gives us free doctors and hospitals.

❻ The Government gives us benefits when we can't help ourselves.

❼ The Government makes sure we are not attacked by other countries.

❽ The Government controls the goods we buy from or sell to other countries.

❾ The Government passes rules which tell businesses what they can do.

Members of Parliament

We saw earlier how in our local areas we can elect **Councillors** to represent us in the **local Council**. The whole country is also divided up into areas called **constituencies**. There are **659** of these altogether in the United Kingdom and **72** of those are in Scotland. Each constituency elects one **MP** to send to the **House of Commons**, which is in London. Soon, too, Scotland will have its own Parliament in Edinburgh and we will elect MSPs to represent us (see page 26).

State of the parties
no. of seats

Labour	Tories	Lib Dem	SNP
56	0	10	6

Edinburgh

Glasgow

Key:
- Labour
- SNP
- Liberal Democrats

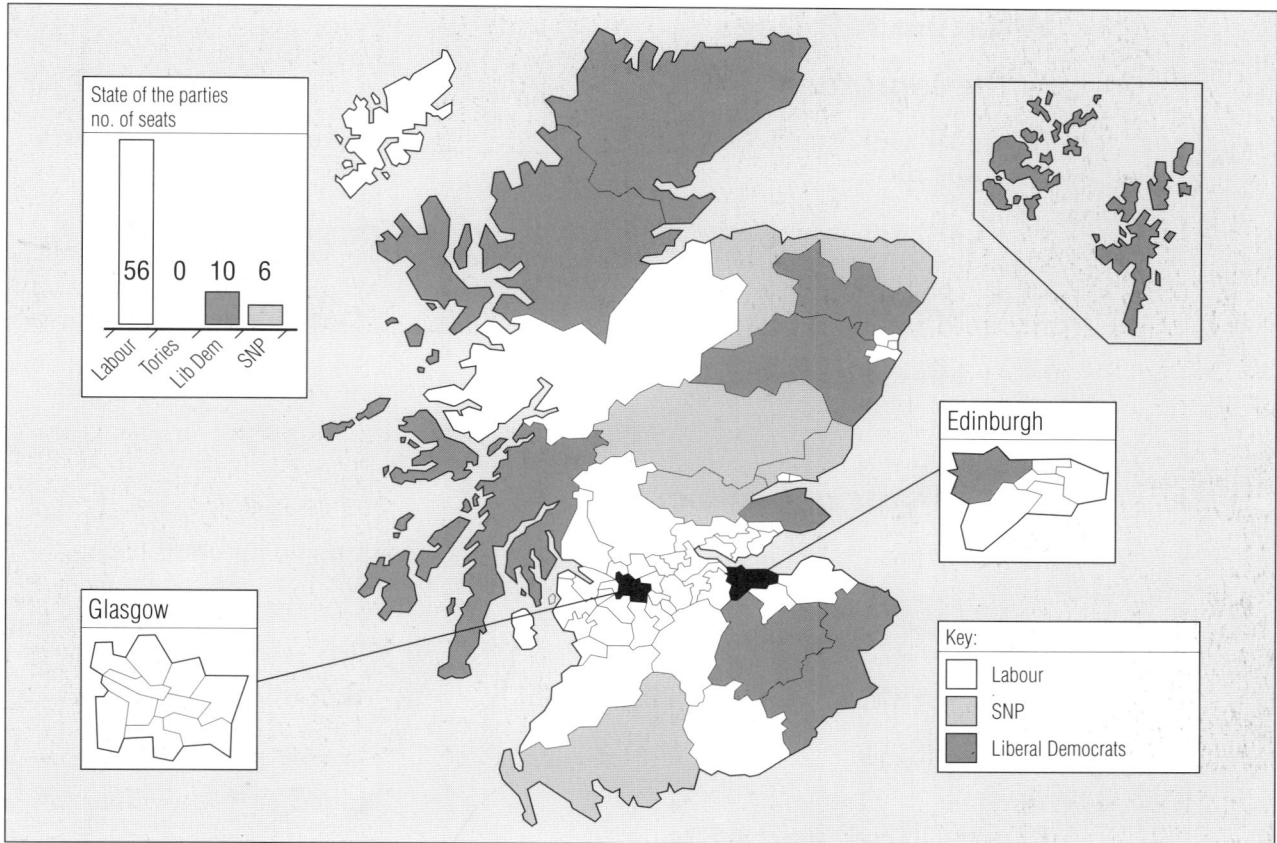

ACTIVITY NINE

Look at the map above showing the results of the 1997 General Election.

❶ Which main party did not win any seats in Scotland?

❷ Which party won the biggest number of seats (constituencies) in Scotland?

What Do MPs Do?

MPs have TWO main jobs to do. First of all, they have to deal with any **problems** that their **constituents** may have in the area they represent. This involves answering **letters**, **meeting** with their constituents in their **surgeries**, and attending various **functions** in their constituency.

Second, since they spend much of their time in the **House of Commons** in London, they have to get involved in the work of **Parliament**. This means that they have to attend **debates** (discussions) on national matters, they can **question Ministers** in the Government, and they have to **vote** on which **laws** they would like to see passed.

ACTIVITY TEN

Copy and complete the sentences overleaf, which show what an MP does:

What an MP Does

In the constituency

❶ An MP will listen to any P __ __ __ __ __ __ that any people in the area have.

❷ An MP will answer any L __ __ __ __ __ __ that people in the area might send.

❸ An MP will meet people in a S __ __ __ __ __ __ to discuss their problems.

❹ An MP will attend lots of different F __ __ __ __ __ __ __ in the local area.

In the House of Commons

❶ An MP will take part in D __ __ __ __ __ __ about many different topics.

❷ An MP can ask M __ __ __ __ __ __ __ in the Government different Q __ __ __ __ __ __ __ __ about matters of concern.

❸ An MP will V __ __ __ on the various L __ __ __ they might want passed

Councillors and MPs

	Councillor	MP	MSP
Elected	locally from a ward	nationally from constituency	from Scottish constituency
Length of term	4 years fixed	up to 5 years	4 years fixed
Works	in the local area	in London – House of Commons	in Edinburgh
Wages	No – but claim expenses	Yes – plus allowances and travel	Yes – plus allowances and travel
Part-time	Yes – can have another job	Yes – can have another job	Yes – can have another job
Holds surgeries	Yes	Yes	Yes
Responsible for	local services	making laws; running the country	Scottish matters
Paid for by	Council Tax and money from UK Parliament	Income Tax, VAT, other taxes	Money from UK Parliament and Scottish Income Tax

* For more information on the Scottish Parliament and the work of Members of the Scottish Parliament see pages 26–27.

We have seen how we can choose a Councillor to represent us at the local level of Government and an MP to represent us at the national level. They both have the job of acting on our behalf to make decisions about the way these areas are run. The table on page 20 shows some facts about the two jobs, and the job of Member of the Scottish Parliament which will be set up in the year 2000.

ACTIVITY ELEVEN

From the table on page 20 find the following information:

★ two things which MPs and Councillors have in common

★ two things which MPs and MSPs will have in common

★ three things which are different for MPs and Councillors

★ two things which Councillors and MSPs will have in common.

Who Can Be an MP?

As an MP's job is a very important one, does this mean you have to be someone special to become an MP? The answer is NO. Apart from lots of good personal qualities, there are only a few conditions for becoming an MP:

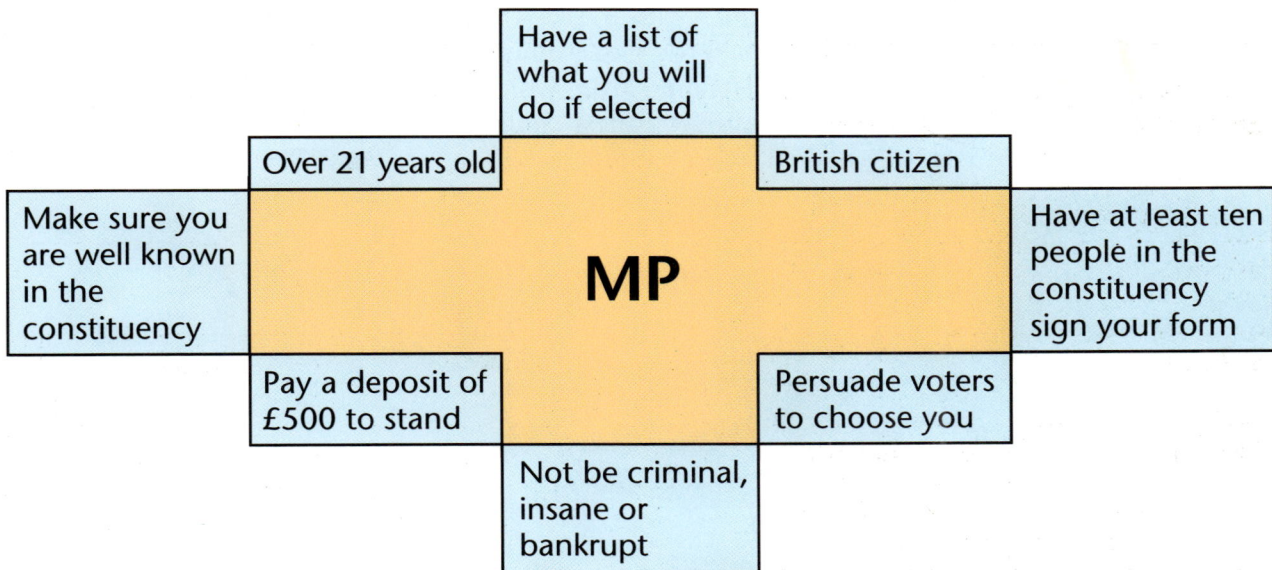

Have a list of what you will do if elected

Over 21 years old

British citizen

Make sure you are well known in the constituency

MP

Have at least ten people in the constituency sign your form

Pay a deposit of £500 to stand

Persuade voters to choose you

Not be criminal, insane or bankrupt

Who Would You Vote For?

Look at the statements listed overleaf which describe different characteristics some people might have. On a separate copy, write yes in the box beside someone you would vote for, and no beside someone you would not vote for.

Black _____   White _____   Young _____

Woman _____   English _____

Old _____   Rich _____   Poor _____

Been to university _____   No certificates _____

Labourer _____   Married with family _____   Has another job _____

ACTIVITY TWELVE

Look at the ones you have written no for, if you had any, and say why you would not vote for these. Try to give sensible reasons for each of your answers. If you did not write no against any, try to say why it did not matter to you who you would vote for.

The General Election 1997

Every five years or so, the people of Britain get a chance to vote for who they think should run the country. They do this by choosing an MP in their own constituency to send to the House of Commons in London. When all of the MPs are chosen, we look at the results to see which party has the most MPs, and this is the party which becomes the Government.

In the 1997 election, the main parties which stood in Scotland were as follows – the pictures are of the current leaders: William Hague (Conservative), Tony Blair, Paddy Ashdown, Alex Salmond.

Fighting for Scotland   Scottish Labour   Liberal Democrats   Scottish National Party

After losing the 1997 General Election, John Major resigned as Leader of the Conservative Party and a new leader, William Hague (above left), was chosen.

Labour 418
Conservative 165
Liberal Democrats 46
Ulster Unionist 10
Scottish National Party 6
Plaid Cymru 4
SDLP 3
Ulster Democratic Unionist 2
United Kingdom Unionist 1
Sinn Fein 2
Independent 1
Referendum Party 0

Key:

	Labour
	Conservative
	Liberal Democrats
	Ulster Unionist
	Scottish National Party
	Plaid Cymru
	SDLP
	Ulster Democratic Unionist
	United Kingdom Unionist
	Sinn Fein
	Independent

Central Scotland	
Labour	31
Liberal Democrats	1

Glasgow	
Labour	10

Tyne and Wear	
Labour	13

Northern Ireland

Greater Manchester, Merseyside, South and West Yorkshire	
Labour	77
Conservative	2
Liberal Democrats	3

West Midlands	
Labour	26
Conservative	4

Greater London	
Labour	56
Conservative	12
Liberal Democrat	6

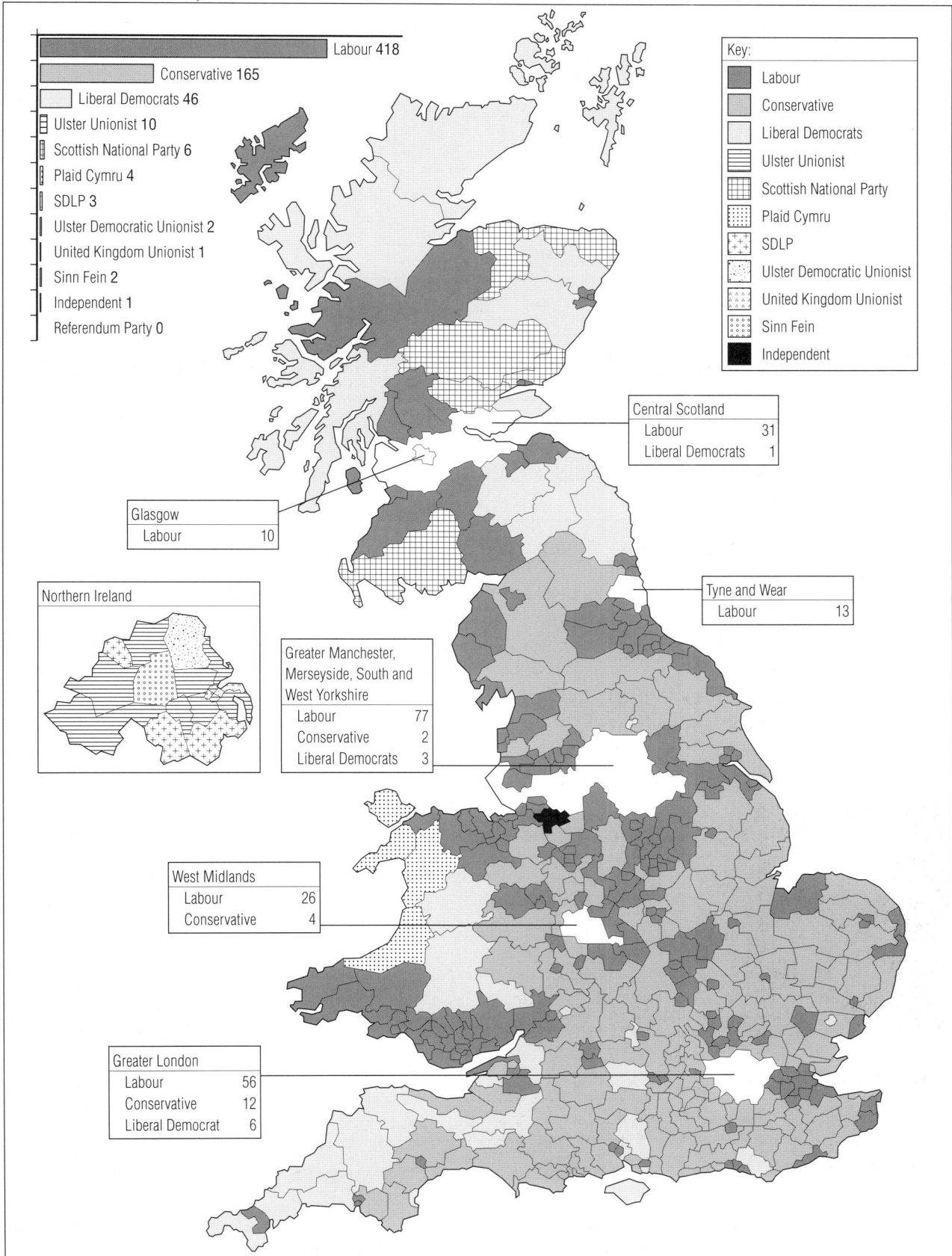

Results of the General Election, 1997

ACTIVITY THIRTEEN

Using the Election 97 map, answer the following questions:

❶ How many Members of Parliament (MPs) are there altogether?

❷ Which party won the election in 1997 and became the Government?

❸ Copy the table below and use the map to help you fill it in.

General Election Results 1997

Party	Seats or MPs
Conservative	
Labour	
Liberal Democrat	
SNP	
Others	
Total	

❹ What majority (how many more MPs than all the others) did the Government have?

❺ How many different parties won seats in the House of Commons?

❻ Find out which constituency you live in, who your MP is, and which party he or she represents.

ACTIVITY FOURTEEN

General Election Results Scotland 1997

Party	Seats or MPs	Votes %
Conservative	0	13
Labour	56	45
Liberal Democrat	10	18
SNP	6	22
Others	0	2
Totals	72	100

❶ Which party won the highest number of seats in Scotland?

❷ Was this the same party which won the election in the whole of the UK?

❸ Were there any parties which won a lot of votes but not a lot of seats?

My Constituency Result 1997

ACTIVITY FIFTEEN

Try to find out the result of the election in your own constituency in 1997. Your teacher will tell you where to look. Fill in a table like the one below.

Party	Candidate	Votes
Conservative		
Labour		
Liberal Democrat		
SNP		
Others		

120 Reasons Why the Commons will Never Be the Same Again (*Daily Record*, 3.5.97)

The House of Commons is a dark, intimidating building. Built in the days when a female MP was unthinkable, it was not designed to cater for women. But this is set to change, thanks to a female revolution sweeping through the Mother of Parliaments. As Labour's landslide enveloped the Tories, the number of women MPs doubled to around 120, changing the face of Parliament. By breaking the magic 100 mark for the first time, they have smashed the world's most exclusive men's club.

Given the spartan facilities that exist for women at Westminster, you'd find it hard to believe that many of the 3000 staff who work at the Commons are female. As well as female Members, catering, cleaning and secretarial staff have had to cope with inadequate amenities. Women presently have to suffer discreetly marked, well-hidden toilets in remote passageways. From committee rooms it's a hike to the nearest ladies and, once there, the facilities are sparse and basic. Places still remain for MPs to hang up their swords, but women have to hunt for places to hang their coats. The House of Commons shop stocks everything from bottles of the best champagne to engraved ashtrays. But ask for a pair of tights or a packet of aspirin and you'll get a pained, quizzical look and pointed in the direction of Walthamstow Market. And it's only now the infamous House of Commons barber will be assisted by a ladies' hairdresser. While there are plenty of bars to choose from and a gun club in the basement, there is no crêche or facilities for mums.

But all that looks set to change with a women's whirlwind about to blow through the dusty Commons corridors. One of those leading the charge is triumphant 47-year-old mother of two Anne McGuire, who saw off Scots Secretary Michael Forsyth in Stirling. She said, "The Labour Party has made a real effort to get more women involved in all levels, and this has been a great bonus. Women have been greatly encouraged and it's paid off."

25

ACTIVITY SIXTEEN

Read the article on page 25.

❶ Why are there likely to be changes made to 'the world's most exclusive men's club' after the 1997 General Election?

❷ What evidence is there that the House of Commons did not cater for women?

❸ What evidence is there that there were a lot of facilities for men?

❹ Why does Anne McGuire think the number of women in the Commons has increased by such a number?

❺ Write a short paragraph to explain what changes we might see to the House of Commons as a result of having so many more women elected.

Scotland's Parliament

| Question One | 'Do you agree there should be a Scottish Parliament?' |
| | *Yes* 74%   *No* 26% |

| Question Two | 'Should the Scottish Parliament have tax varying powers?' |
| | *Yes* 63%   *No* 37% |

On 11 September 1997, the Scottish people voted to have their own Parliament in Edinburgh. The first elections for the Scottish Parliament will be held in 1999 and it will meet for the first time in 2000.

Scotland will elect 129 members to the new Parliament and its leader will be called First Minister. Scotland will continue to remain part of the United Kingdom, and the UK Parliament in Westminster will continue to make laws which affect the whole of the United Kingdom. Scotland will still elect MPs to the UK Parliament, but the number will be cut from the present 72 members. This will be decided later, when the new Scottish Parliament is up and running.

Some of the important matters affecting people in Scotland which the Scottish Parliament will deal with are:

Health	Education	Training
Local government	Transport	Social work
Housing	Legal system	Sport

The money to pay for these services would come in two ways:

★ The UK Parliament would give the Scottish Parliament a large sum of money each year (possibly around £15 billion). The Scottish Parliament will decide how this money would be spent.

★ People in Scotland voted for their Parliament to have tax powers. This means people who live and work in Scotland might pay more or less income tax (up to 3 pence more or less in each pound sterling).

ACTIVITY SEVENTEEN

Read the information on Scotland's Parliament on page 26, and answer the following questions.

❶ What were the two main questions the Scottish people were asked to vote on?

❷ On the first question, what percentage voted yes and how many voted no?

❸ On the second question, what percentage voted yes and how many voted no?

❹ Why do you think fewer people voted yes to question two than to question one?

❺ How would you have voted? Give reasons for your answer, and say whether or not you think a Scottish Parliament is a good idea.

❻ Look at the table on page 26 – on the powers of the Scottish Parliament. Can you think of any important powers which the UK Parliament at Westminster will continue to have?

❼ Make a collection of newspaper articles from now until the new Scottish Parliament is set up in 2000, and keep an up-to-date Scrapbook.

Voting in Elections

When you become 18, you will be entitled to vote in elections for Councillors, MPs and MSPs. You should know what you have to do when you vote. There are a number of different stages you have to go through to take part or **participate** in elections. These stages are listed in the boxes below, but they are all jumbled up.

ACTIVITY EIGHTEEN

Copy each of the stages in voting from page 28 on to a sheet of paper. Cut out the different stages in voting, number them in order of how they should happen, and show them to your teacher. If you have numbered them correctly, you should stick them in your notebook.

You are handed
a ballot paper.
A

You put a cross
on the ballot paper.
B

You arrive at the
polling station.
C

You give your name
to the polling station.
D

The votes are collected
and counted.
E

You go into the
polling booth.
F

You put the ballot paper
in the box.
G

The polling station
closes for the day.
H

Your name is crossed
off by the clerk.
I

ACTIVITY NINETEEN

In groups, you should discuss why it is important to have a secret ballot. Try to think of a number of reasons.

Participation

We now know that Britain is a democracy and that our elected representatives should listen to our views and opinions and try their best to represent all of us. Sometimes, though, this will not be possible, as you can't please all of the people all of the time. So perhaps trying to represent the majority is a good idea – as long as minority views and opinions are not ignored.

As we live in a democracy, we can participate in making decisions and try to influence our elected representatives. If the only way we could participate was to have a vote every four or five years, we would not be doing very much, would we?

Ways in Which We can Participate

We can participate, however, in lots of other ways and try to make our views and opinions known. We can do this either by becoming more involved in politics, or more simply by taking advantage of our democratic rights and freedoms.

Here are some ideas of the ways in which we can become more involved in how decisions are made:

Voting in elections

Writing letters to Councillors, MPs and MSPs

Visiting Councillors, MPs and MSPs' surgeries

Standing as a candidate

Protests and demonstrations

Signing petitions

Writing to newspapers

Joining a pressure group

Joining a political party

Pressure Groups

An important way you can participate and become involved in helping to change the society in which you live is by joining a pressure group.

A 'pressure group' is an organised group of people, sometimes from different political parties, who share a belief in one thing and who try to pressure the Government into supporting their cause or changing the law to help their cause.

Joining a pressure group is popular in the United Kingdom, particularly among younger people who want to become involved in trying to change society and who may not be old enough to join a political party or to vote.

You probably know something already about pressure groups, even if you did not know that is what they are called! You or your parents may even be a member of one or more pressure groups.

Here are some examples of charities in the UK which you may have heard of. Many of these charities are pressure groups.

SHELTER

FRIENDS of the earth
for the planet for people

FRIENDS OF THE EARTH

AMNESTY

CHRISTIAN AID
AN OFFICIAL AGENCY OF BRITISH AND IRISH CHURCHES

OXFAM
UNITED KINGDOM AND IRELAND

OXFAM

As we move into the 21st century, a number of different pressure groups are trying to protect the environment or help the poor and hungry in under-developed countries. Sometimes a pressure group will receive more publicity and support if it recruits a famous person like an actor, pop star or sports personality to help promote its cause. Pressure groups rely on publicity to highlight their cause, perhaps to embarass the Government and persuade politicians to change the law. They also rely on good publicity to encourage people to donate money to them, although they may also raise money through membership subscriptions (you pay to join and to remain a member) or by sales of products like leaflets, badges, posters, magazines and perhaps even CDs and videos.

Many people who are not otherwise involved in politics are members of pressure groups and argue that pressure groups are good for a democracy because they allow ordinary people to help shape the society in which they live. Pressure groups also highlight issues which sometimes politicians either do not wish to tackle or cannot agree on.

Others do not like pressure groups and think they are a bad idea. They argue that not all pressure groups have the same power and influence and it is the big, powerful ones which get their way, leaving the smaller ones with little say. Some people also say that because pressure groups, unlike politicians, are not elected, we cannot remove the power and influence they may have and that in a democracy it is elected people who should make decisions.

ACTIVITY TWENTY

❶ Explain in your own words what you think a pressure group is.

❷ Are you a member of a pressure group? If so, which one? If not, is there a pressure group you think you may support? Give reasons for your answer.

❸ Why do you think pressure groups may be attractive to young people?

❹ List three ways in which pressure groups may raise money.

❺ Look back to page 30 at the examples of pressure groups. Can you add any others to the list?

❻ Can you give any examples of:
   • an actor
   • a sports personality
   • a pop star
   • a TV personality
   who has helped a pressure group?
Write a few sentences saying what he/she has done.

❼ Read this statement: 'Pressure groups are not good for our democracy.'
   Do you agree with this statement? Give reasons for your answer.

8 Over the next week or so collect as many items as you can to do with pressure groups – it could be badges, leaflets, posters, photographs, newspaper clippings or magazine articles. You could perhaps find out the address of a pressure group which interests you and write to them for information.

Ask your teacher to select a sample of these items and make a class display.

Rights and Responsibilities

We must remember that our individual freedom to make our own views and opinions known, must not mean that other people's freedoms are taken away. Sometimes this can be difficult. We must also remember that while we have rights in a democracy, we also have responsibilities – and we must always obey the law. (You should be very clear by now about why we need laws.) One of our rights in a democracy, however, is to change the law if we think it is a bad law. We can participate in persuading our respresentatives to change the law, as long as we do it peacefully.

So there are lots of opportunities in a democracy for us to participate. We have lots of **rights**, but we also have lots of **responsibilities**.

Here is a table listing some rights and responsibilities each of us has in a democracy:

Rights	Responsibilities
To vote in elections	To use our vote
To demonstrate	To do so peacefully
To have freedom of speech	To listen to others
To express an opinion	To respect other people's opinions
To join a pressure group	To respect other groups' rights
To change the law	To obey the law until it changes

ACTIVITY TWENTY-ONE

Take each of the responsibilities above in turn and explain in your own words why these are important. Can you think of any other important rights and responsibilities we may have?

Groups – How Do They Affect Us?

Types of Family

In our society, we belong to many different kinds of groups. We are sitting in a group at the moment, aren't we? The most important type of group for all of us, particularly for young people, is the family. Despite all of the times we may disagree with our parents, and feel that they make unnecessary rules for us, the family group is one of the most important influences on our life. But, what is a family?

ACTIVITY ONE

Write down in your notebook the name of each family member **who lives in your house**. Keep it simple. For example:

James (Dad), Margaret (Mum), Robert (brother) and Susan (me).

Now compare your family list with others in the class. Some will have lots of names, others fewer. Some may have Gran or Grandad on the list. Others may have one parent, or stepbrothers and sisters. There are many different types of family. We are going to look at four types of family in our society today.

The Nuclear Family	The Extended Family
This family consists of Mum, Dad and children, the typical family of two generations living in the same house.	This family is like the nuclear family, but with a grandparent or grandparents living in the same house. This would be a family of at least three generations.
The Second Family	**The One-Parent Family**
This is a family where Mum or Dad has married for a second time and there may be children from the first marriage, and also perhaps children from the second marriage.	This is a family where only one parent (Mum or Dad), possibly after a separation, divorce or the death of the other partner, stays in the house with the children.

ACTIVITY TWO

❶ Which type of family best describes your own?

❷ Which type of family would you most like to live in? Give reasons.

❸ Can you think of at least THREE advantages of living in

a) a nuclear family

b) an extended family?

Remember that when we are talking about families we are really only looking at people who live in the same house. You will have lots of other members of your family if you count all your cousins, aunts, uncles and other relatives.

Have Families Changed over the Years?

A hundred years ago, the typical family in Britain was very different from what we see today. Most families were very large, with possibly ten or twelve children, and fewer people had grandparents as, on average, people did not live as long. The average life expectancy for a Victorian mother was under 50 years. Nowadays families are much smaller and people tend to live longer. (Did you know that on average, women live longer than men!) The average size of a family in Britain going into the 21st century is 2.4 children; women live to an average age of 79, with men only averaging 75.

ACTIVITY THREE

❶ Can you think of any reasons why:

a) family size is smaller than 100 years ago?

b) women now live a lot longer than they did 100 years ago?

c) women live longer on average than men?

❷ Ask your parents to describe to you their family when they were children. Can you find at least two similarities and two differences from your own?

❸ Why do you think the nuclear family of two parents and children is less common today than when your parents were children?

❹ Conduct a class survey and draw a pie-chart or bar graph showing the different types of family of your class members.

How are Families Likely to Change?

Although the nuclear family is often thought of as the 'typical' family in Britain, it is less common than many people think. A family of two parents with children under 16 represents less than 25% (a quarter) of all families in the UK.

Single-parent families with children make up 22% of all families in the UK. The table below showing the number of marriages in Britain may help us to see how families may look in the future.

Marriages in the UK 1992 (Source: 'Annual Abstract of Statistics', 1995)

Type of person	Number (1992)
Single men	258,567
Divorced men	87,419
Widowers	10,027
Single women	260,252
Divorced women	86,361
Widows	9,400
First marriage (for both)	222,142
First marriage (for either)	74,535
Re-marriage (for both)	59,336

Marriages in the UK

In 1992, the total number of marriages in the UK was 356,013 and the total number of divorces was 175,100. Marriage is still very popular despite the rising number of divorces.

Single-Parent Families

There can be a number of different types of single-parent families also. Some of them perhaps began as nuclear families but the parents separated or mum or dad died. The figures below show the different types of single-parent families in the UK in the 1990s.

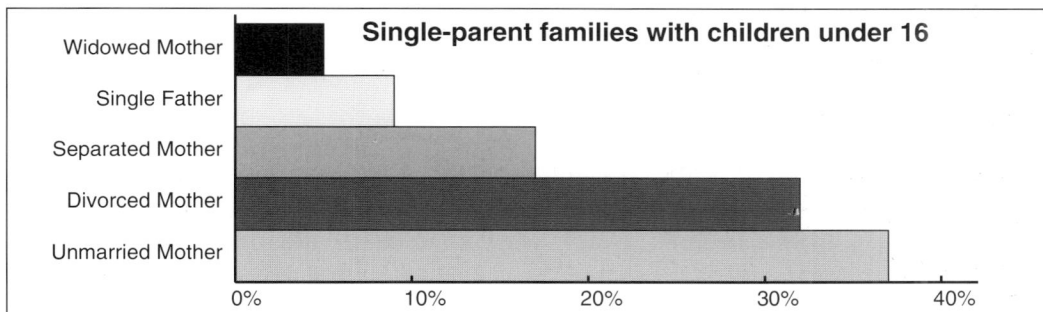

(Source: General Household Survey 1995)

Age of Marriage

Most families begin when a couple decide to get married and have children. More than three-quarters (75%) of all children born in the UK are born to married couples. So what do you think is the most popular age to get married? Eighteen? Twenty-one? Forty? Is it the same for men and women? The figures on the next page show us what age people get married at.

Marriages in the UK by Age and Gender

(Source: Annual Abstract of Statistics 1995).

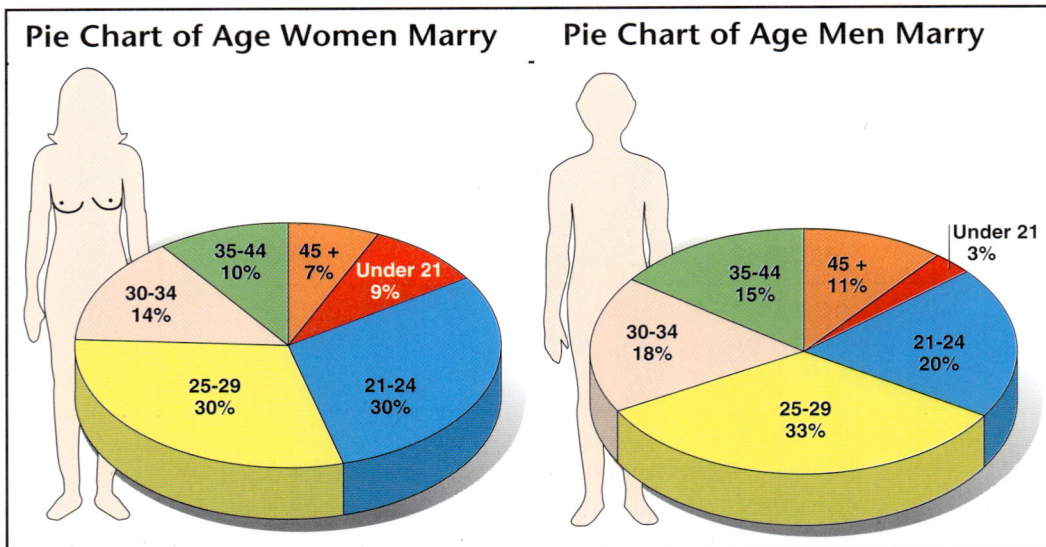

Pie Chart of Age Women Marry

- 35-44 10%
- 45 + 7%
- Under 21 9%
- 30-34 14%
- 25-29 30%
- 21-24 30%

Pie Chart of Age Men Marry

- 35-44 15%
- 45 + 11%
- Under 21 3%
- 30-34 18%
- 25-29 33%
- 21-24 20%

ACTIVITY FOUR

❶ Ask your mum or dad what age they were when they married. Were they typical of the ages of marriage shown for 1995?

❷ Using the figures in the tables above, answer the following questions 'True' or 'False':

a) The largest group of single-parent families is where the mother is divorced.

b) Single-father families are as common as divorced-mother families.

c) The most popular age range for men getting married is 25–29.

d) Most married women are married before they reach 30 years old.

e) Men on average are older than women when they marry.

Why do We Need Families?

Food and shelter

Looking after children when they are young

Teaching right from wrong	Looking after old members of the family

Every society has family groups. Some may be very different from our own type of family, but the family as a social group is very important to us all. The illustrations above and on the previous page give some examples of important needs that the family helps us to meet.

A family is very important in teaching children how to become good citizens and how to behave in society. Perhaps now we can understand better why we need rules and laws, and why learning to behave in different groups is important.

The family is often said to be the most basic and most important unit in society, and although other groups and organisations, like school or youth clubs or sports teams, help us learn different skills or abilities, it is really the family which teaches us, from a very early age, how to behave in the society in which we grow up. Believe it or not, two of the most complicated and difficult things you will ever have to learn in your whole life, have already been taught to you by your family – learning to walk, and learning to talk.

Socialisation

This type of learning from your family is called **socialisation**, and it is exactly the same way animals learn. They, and you, learn by watching parents and copying their example. A fledgling bird learns to fly by watching its parents. A duckling learns to swim by copying its mother, and a lion cub is taught to hunt by the adults in the pack.

So families teach children the skills they need to survive in their own society, and are a great influence on the way children behave. Families also teach children important values, like trust and sharing and a sense of responsibility – all of the things that help children grow up into responsible and good citizens. These things are so important that they are often called **'family values'**.

The Family and Money

The family has a very important economic role to play for its members. It has to provide food and shelter and money so they can enjoy a good standard of living. This is normally done by a parent or both parents working and bringing a wage into the house. Everyone needs money nowadays, for rent or a mortgage, food, clothing, heating, holidays, leisure and sports, and some other luxuries now and again. Perhaps you or your older brothers or sisters have part-time jobs like a paper round which help out with the family money. Running a home and a family is an expensive business, especially when you pester your parents for extra pocket money or for designer clothes or CDs and videos. Just as there are different types of family, there are also different types of income coming into family homes. Some families are very well off, and others are very poor by comparison.

What things may affect how well off a family is or how poor a family is?

What Types of Family Do Better?

All families want to have as high a standard of living as possible, but for some families this can be very difficult. In a two-parent nuclear family, there could be two wages coming into the house. Both parents could work either full-time or part-time. In a single-parent family, there will only be one parent bringing in a wage at most. It is too simple to say, however, that nuclear families are better off than single-parent families. Lots of other factors have to be taken into account, like unemployment, type of job, wage rates, number of children, and so on. Figures do suggest, however, that single-parent families tend to be poorer, and a lot of this probably has to do with the fact that the parent cannot work as there are children to be looked after.

The figures in the pie-charts below show us how the different types of family get their money.

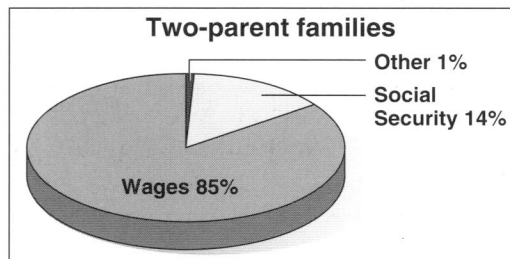

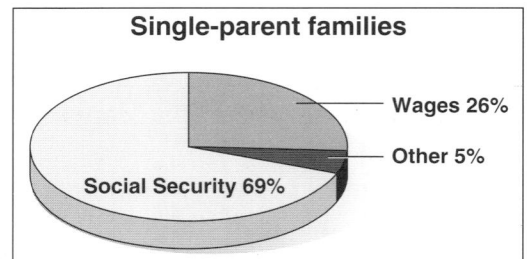

Two-parent families
Other 1%
Social Security 14%
Wages 85%

Single-parent families
Wages 26%
Other 5%
Social Security 69%

Wages – money from a job or jobs.
Social Security – money paid by the Government to families on a low income to help them improve their standard of living.
Other – a variety of things like savings or money paid by an absent parent as child support, or help from a charity.
(Source: Adapted from 'Social Trends', 1995)

Types of Job

Another reason why parents in single-parent families tend to be less well off than others is that the single parent is usually the mother, and women are more often found in jobs which are low paid. The table below helps to show this.

Low-paid jobs in the UK (Source: Adapted from 'Low Pay Unit', 1995)

Job	Hourly rate (£)
1. Waitress	3.46
2. Childcare	3.49
3. Hairdresser	3.64
4. Barmaid	3.68
5. Laundry worker	3.73
6. Kitchen work	3.82
7. Sewing machinist	3.96
8. Catering	4.02
9. Cleaner/domestic	4.12
10. Nursing	4.22

Single mothers are also more likely to work part-time and therefore will earn less. In 1995, 44% of all women workers in the UK worked part-time compared to only 7% of men.

Difficulties Facing Single Parents

There are lots of reasons why single parents find it difficult to find a job, apart from the usual problems in being unemployed. The diagram below shows some of these reasons.

Looking after the children	No weekend work	No shift work – start after 9.00 am finish by 3.00 pm
Lack of training or qualifications	Can't afford the time or cost of travelling	Can't afford a childminder

Family and Income and Children

The type of family a child comes from and the amount of money the family has to spend can obviously affect the standard of living a child has. But these things can also affect other important aspects of a child's life. This is shown in the illustrations below.

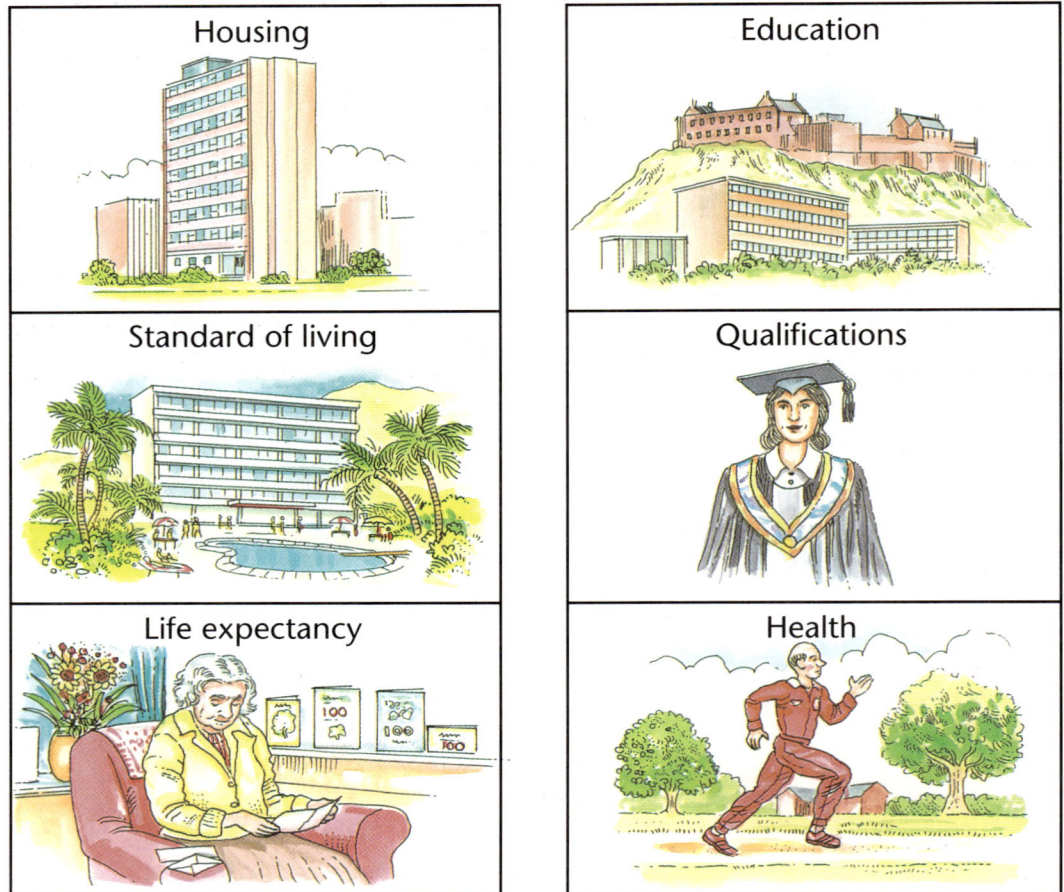

Housing	Education
Standard of living	Qualifications
Life expectancy	Health

Standard of Living of Families

Different incomes mean different standards of living. Some groups in society are better off than others. A family's standard of living will depend on a lot of different things:

Luxuries	Parents' job	Savings
Type of house	Education and qualifications	Number of children

The type of job is probably the most important single factor in deciding your family's standard of living (unless you win the Lottery!). We have already seen some figures on low-paid jobs done by women. Here are some figures showing average weekly earnings for men and women in full-time jobs in the UK in 1995.

Average Weekly Earnings (Source: 'Employment Gazette', 1995 – adjusted)

Type of job	Weekly wage (£)	
	Women	Men
Managers and administrators	365	526
Professional occupations	419	503
Technical occupations	340	444
Clerical/secretarial	234	276
Craft	186	314
Sales	208	315
Machine operators	200	295
Others	174	247

ACTIVITY FIVE

❶ Try to find an example of a job in each of the categories listed above. Your teacher will help you with some.

❷ If your mum or dad has a job, try to find out in what category in the table it is.

❸ In groups, discuss why you think women are paid less than men. Do you think this is fair? Which type of family would this affect most?

Good Education – Good Job?

Generally, the more qualifications a person has and the more skill that is required for a job, the higher the wages. This is not always the case. Pop stars, sportsmen, television presenters and celebrities can all earn thousands of pounds a week.

For most families, however, their standard of living will depend on the types of job done by parents and how much they earn. Despite the big differences in standards of living, every family in the UK should be entitled to a basic decent standard of living which gives them all the necessities in life. These necessities include things like rent for housing, food, clothing, heating, and some leisure.

Lots of families can only afford the necessities and don't have much left over for any luxuries. Many of us have these luxuries and take them for granted: things like CD players, holidays, car, videos etc. Families on low incomes are often said to be 'on the breadline' or 'on the poverty line', which means that they only have enough money to survive and not much more.

Rich and Poor

The families that are said to be below the poverty line are helped by the Government. The Government gives them a number of benefits, or money help, which allows them to pay for the basics that they need to survive. Almost 20% of the money the Government spends on benefits each year goes to families who are near the poverty line. Benefits are needed because not everyone in the UK has a decent standard of living, and the wealth of the country is not evenly distributed. This means that lots of people only have a little money to live on, while a few people have lots of money. The richest 1% of the UK population have almost 20% of the country's wealth. The richest 10% of the population have almost 50% of the country's wealth – and the poorest 50% of the population have less than 10% of the country's wealth. Put simply, this means that there are many more poor people in our society than rich people, and amongst the poorest groups you will find lots of single parents, elderly and unemployed people.

Women and the Family

In your grandparents' time, it was probably the case that your grandmother stayed at home to look after the house and the children, while your grandfather went out to work. He was seen as the 'breadwinner' in the family, earning the money to pay for the family's needs. His wife had the job of looking after him and the rest of the family. Nowadays, with an increase in the number of one-parent families and with more women going out to work, in many ways this has changed. Or has it?

ACTIVITY SEVEN

❶ Look at the table showing jobs done around the house, copy it into your notebook and tick which are done by a woman in your house, and which are done by a man.

Activity	Mainly man	Mainly woman	Either
Washing and ironing			
Making evening meal			
Shopping			
Household repairs			
Looking after sick child			
Doing dishes			
Gardening			
Decorating the house			

❷ What would happen in your house if it was suggested that the jobs be switched around?

❸ What would you like to see happen in your own house when you become an adult?

Women and Careers

When girls are at school and considering their options for future careers, it might be expected by some people that they should go into certain types of job. If you look around, you will probably be able to see that women are doing certain types of job and men are doing other types. It might be thought unusual if a girl, or a boy, decided to go into a career that was normally full of people of the opposite sex.

ACTIVITY EIGHT

Look at the list of jobs in the table overleaf, copy it into your notebook and tick whether you would expect to see a man or a woman, or either, doing that job.

43

Job	Man	Woman	Job	Man	Woman
Receptionist			Model		
Bricklayer			Surgeon		
Nurse			Teacher		
Pilot			Bank manager		
Cleaner			HGV driver		
Fire-fighter			Farmer		
Gas fitter			Window cleaner		
Beauty Therapist			Roadsweeper		
Doctor			Secretary		
MP			Canteen assistant		

❶ How do you think people would react to seeing someone in an 'unusual' job?

❷ How would your friends and family react if you chose a job normally associated with the opposite sex?

❸ Would you consider taking one of these types of job?

Ethnic Minority Families

People have been coming to live in Britain for hundreds of years, from the Romans to the Vikings and Normans a long time ago, and more recently in the last century, the Irish. Since the Second World War in 1945, other groups of people have come to settle in Britain, like Indians and Pakistanis and people from the Caribbean. These people have all brought their own cultures, languages, religions and customs with them, and this has made Britain a multicultural society, where each person has the right to keep their own customs. Many people from Britain's minority groups have not been made to feel as welcome as the earlier arrivals, however, especially if their skins were black. Read the newspaper article overleaf and answer the questions which follow.

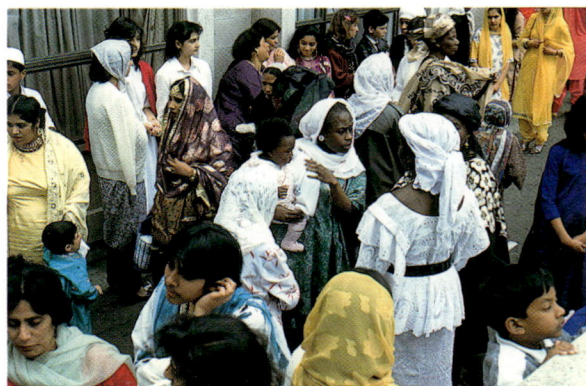

Ethnic Groups to get Panic Alarms

Ethnic minorities in Dundee are to be issued with panic alarms in a pioneering scheme to combat racist attacks. The phone-based system will allow a victim of racism to press a panic button in their home for connection to the 24-hour service. A dedicated operator will receive the call and will be able to contact the police and the victim's family or friends from information stored in a database. Vulnerable members of ethnic groups, including the elderly and those who cannot speak English, will be a priority for issue with the alarms.

The system has been proposed by Tayside Racial Equality Council, which is working to consolidate a decline in racial attacks in the region over the last two years. Racial incidents in Tayside dropped from 134 in 1994 to 123 last year but there has been concern in Dundee about the number of attacks, which stood at 98 last year. However, the scheme was denounced last night by Mr Bill Walker, Conservative MP for North Tayside. He said: 'It's one of these things that are political correctness going mad and we should put a stop to it. The more you draw attention to these things, the more you get copycats. There's every likelihood that pensioners could ask for panic buttons because more pensioners find themselves being mugged than any other group.' He added: 'I personally can see no reason why any particular group should be singled out and public money being spent in this way. I think this is a mistake and it looks like positive discrimination.'

The MP's remarks were condemned by the ethnic community in the city. Jyoti Hazra, a former chairman of the Asian Action Group, said, 'Mr Walker is talking nonsense. He does not understand the problems faced by the ethnic minorities in Dundee.'

A working group from Tayside Racial Equality Council is putting together the fine details of the scheme, which it is hoped will be launched in August. It is thought that 25 people will take part in the service when it is launched and it is estimated that each alarm could cost about £150.

Mr John White, chief officer of the Racial Equality Council, explained: 'To the best of our knowledge, this scheme will be the first of its kind in Scotland.'

(Source: The *Herald*, 18.1.96)

ACTIVITY NINE

❶ What are the authorities in Dundee proposing to try to stop racist attacks?

❷ Why does Bill Walker, North Tayside Conservative MP, oppose the plan?

❸ How does the ethnic community reply to Mr Walker's claims?

❹ How much does the scheme cost, and how many people will take part?

❺ What do you think is meant by the phrase 'positive discrimination'?

❻ Do you think that Scotland is a 'multicultural society'?

The Elderly and the Family

In Scotland today there are over 900,000 people of pensionable age, that is, men over 65 and women over 60. They account for 18% of the population in Scotland and their numbers are getting larger all the time. The average life expectancy in Scotland is about 75 years of age, and it too is increasing. The chances are that you will not only have fit and active grandparents, but that you might also still have your great-grandparents. Hopefully, if they live close to you, you will see them quite often and no doubt they will spoil you.

Some elderly people, however, are not fit and active enough to be able to live on their own. They might have to move house because the garden is too big, or because there is an upstairs that they can't manage, or because they simply can't get about as easily now. For many of these elderly people, most of the help is provided by their family, friends or neighbours. The idea that families 'dump' their grannies into homes is not true. Only 1.8% of elderly people in Scotland (16,107) are in residential care of some kind, that is, residential homes, nursing homes or hospitals; whereas over 570,000 people in Scotland, that's about one in ten, are caring for an elderly person. Many of these carers are looking after elderly relatives or neighbours, but there are also people caring for their husband or wife. 30% of carers are over 65.

ACTIVITY TEN

Answer the following questions in your notebooks:

❶ How many elderly people are there in Scotland, and what percentage of the population is this?

❷ Why do you think the life expectancy of people in Scotland is increasing?

❸ How often do you see your elderly relatives? Do you see them as often as you should, and do you do as much for them as you could?

❹ Is it true that people like to put their elderly relatives into homes?

Care in the Community

Since so many elderly people are still living in their own homes, or are being looked after by families and friends, the idea of 'care in the community' has been developed to make sure that these elderly people and their carers can continue to live this way for as long as they wish. Care in the community involves a wide range of services to help these elderly people. The diagram below shows some of the services that are available.

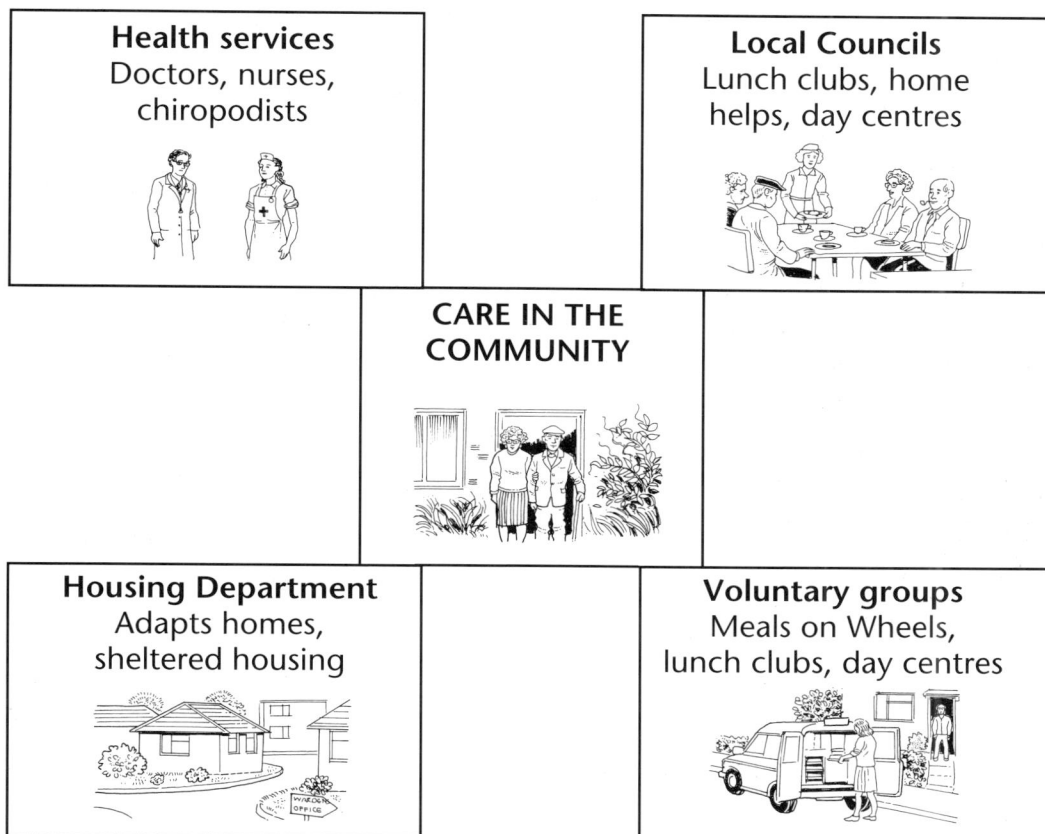

Health services
Doctors, nurses, chiropodists

Local Councils
Lunch clubs, home helps, day centres

CARE IN THE COMMUNITY

Housing Department
Adapts homes, sheltered housing

Voluntary groups
Meals on Wheels, lunch clubs, day centres

ACTIVITY ELEVEN

Take each of the areas of care in the community listed in the diagram and write a few sentences for each in your notebook, explaining how people in the community can help to meet the needs of elderly people.

❶ Should the Government be doing more to look after the elderly?

❷ What could be done to make living conditions better for the elderly in Scotland?

Find out how much the 'old age pension' is for single pensioners and married couples.

Try to find similar figures in other countries in Europe. Do any of these figures surprise you?

4 The Media – How Does It Influence Us?

Methods of Communicating

When we talk about the **media** (sometimes called the **mass media**), we mean ways in which lots of information can be passed on to large numbers of people very quickly. Let's think of an example in our own school.

Imagine the head teacher has decided to close the school an hour early. How might this information be passed on to pupils and teachers? Here are some ways this might be done:

★ Ask every pupil to come to the head teacher's office to be told about it.

★ Get the head teacher to go round every class and tell all the pupils.

★ Call an assembly for all of the pupils and tell them there.

★ Ask some senior pupils to take notes around the classes.

★ Use the school loudspeaker system if there is one.

ACTIVITY ONE

❶ What might be the disadvantages of each of these methods?

❷ Which method do you think is the best one, and why?

How Quickly Can We Find Out?

The problem above is that news would have to be passed on as quickly as possible so that everyone found out about it. This is exactly what has to be done with the media. It gives us, the public, news and information quickly, and it can reach everybody at the same time.

When we talk about the media, all we are talking about are those methods of communication we use every day of our lives. Here are some examples of the main types:

Television

Radio

MEDIA

Newspapers

Computers

Radio

Radio is just over 100 years old. It was invented by a man called Marconi, who sent the first radio message in 1895. It became very popular from the 1920s onwards and played a very important part in the Second World War. From the 1960s, transistor radios became very popular. (Your mum and dad probably had a 'tranny'.) Radio is not so important, at least in this country, as it was 40 or 50 years ago. Can you think why? You probably listen to the radio only to hear pop music or some local news, or when you are travelling in a car. See if you can complete the following activity:

ACTIVITY TWO

Try to complete a copy of the table overleaf. (Clue – look in the radio guide in a newspaper. The first five on your list should be national stations and the last two should be local stations.)

Name of radio station	Frequency (where to find it!)
1.	
2.	
3.	
4.	
5.	
6.	
7.	

Which Types of Radio Programmes do You Listen to?

The table below shows some of the types of radio programme you might listen to. Tick those types you might listen to during a normal week, and answer the questions below the table.

ACTIVITY THREE

Copy the table below into your notebook and fill it in.

Programme	Tick
Pop music	
Classical music	
News/local news	
Quiz programmes	
Plays/stories	
Sports	
Adverts	
Other	

❶ How many of the different types of radio programme did you tick?

❷ Can you think of any advantages that radio might have over television?

❸ Can you think of any disadvantages?

❹ How many radios are there in your house? (Don't forget hi-fis and CD players which may have radios.)

Television

Television is not as old as radio. In fact, it was around 1925 that a Scotsman called John Logie Baird invented television. From the 1950s, television developed very quickly. At first, there was only one channel, BBC1, and it was only in monochrome (black and white). ITV, Independent Television, came along in 1958, and BBC2 started in 1967. Colour TVs became popular in the 1970s, and Channel 4 began in 1982. Channel 5 joined these other channels in 1997. These five channels are all to be seen on normal television, and are sometimes called the terrestrial channels, as their transmitters are all on land. Some of you will now have either cable or satellite television, which can give you 40 or 50 channels to choose from. Television has come a long way in a few short years.

ACTIVITY FOUR

❶ How many televisions are there in your house? Are they all colour?

❷ Do you have a television in your room?

❸ Do you have satellite or cable TV?

❹ What advantages does television have over radio?

❺ Do you prefer television or radio? Give a reason for your answer.

How do Television Channels Get Their Money?

You may have noticed that there are no adverts on BBC1 and BBC2, but that all of the other channels have them. This is because the BBC gets the money it needs to make programmes from the television **licence fee**. Everyone who owns a television set must pay this licence fee each year, and all of the money goes to the BBC.

Find out how much the television licence fee is.

The other, independent channels get their money from companies who advertise on TV. Satellite and cable TV charge a monthly subscription from their viewers.

Find out how much it costs per month to watch these channels.

Some big sporting events on satellite and cable cost extra to watch. This is called pay-view television.

BBC1 and BBC2	Money comes from the licence fee which is paid by everyone who has a television set.
ITV, CH4, CH5	Money comes from those companies which advertise their products on the commercial channels.
SKY/BSB, CABLE	Money comes from those people who pay their monthly subscriptions to these companies, from adverts and from pay-view.

Regional Programmes

With the terrestrial television channels (BBC1, BBC2, ITV and Channels 4 and 5), not everyone in the UK gets the same programmes at the same time. BBC1 makes special programmes for Scotland, for example, and you can recognise these by the sign at the start which says 'BBC Scotland'. Local news programmes, like 'Reporting Scotland', or sports programmes, like 'Sportscene', are made especially for viewers in Scotland.

Independent Television has special channels for different parts of the UK. The three Scottish channels are called Scottish Television, Grampian, and Borders. Where you live will tell you which of the three you will get. If you live in Central Scotland (e.g. in Glasgow or Edinburgh) you will get Scottish Television or STV. If you live in Aberdeen or Inverness, you will get Grampian. If you live in Dumfries or Berwick, you will get Borders.

The ITV Regions

There are a total of 15 ITV regional companies which cover the whole of the UK. Each of them makes their own programmes, and you can tell which ones by the logo at the start of the programme. They show not only their own programmes, but ones which they have bought from other stations. 'Coronation Street', for example, is made by Granada and sold all over the UK. They also buy programmes from abroad. 'Home and Away', for example, is bought from Australia. Some programmes like the BBC News and ITV's 'News at Ten' go out at the same time each day and can be seen by everyone in the UK no matter where they stay.

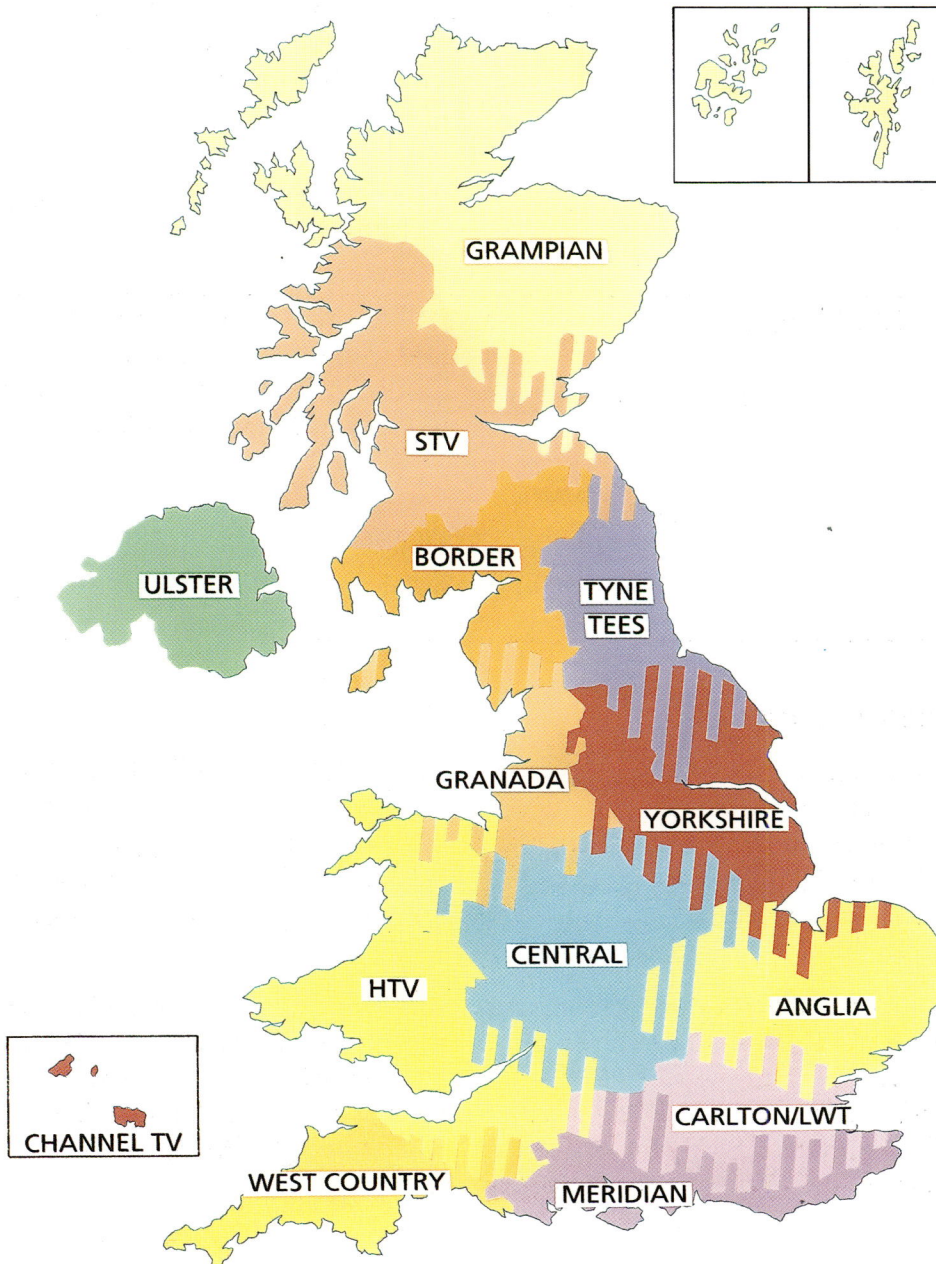

GRAMPIAN

STV

BORDER

ULSTER

TYNE TEES

GRANADA

YORKSHIRE

CENTRAL

HTV

ANGLIA

CARLTON/LWT

CHANNEL TV

WEST COUNTRY

MERIDIAN

ACTIVITY FIVE

❶ Can you find out what logo or symbol is used for each of the companies listed and which area of the UK the company covers?

❷ Can you list the names of some of the programmes made by these stations?

❸ Can you think of any other programmes which might be seen by everyone in the UK at the same time?

❹ Find a page taken from a daily newspaper which shows what programmes are on the main TV channels on a normal day. Use this to answer the questions below.

Which programmes, if any, are made by the following stations:

a) BBC Scotland;

e) Thames TV;

b) Scottish Television;

f) Central;

c) Granada;

g) Carlton;

d) Yorkshire/Tyne-Tees;

h) ITN?

Which programmes, if any, have been bought from:

a) America;

b) Australia?

❺ List THREE regional variations for BBC1.

Satellite and Cable Television

Satellite and cable television gives us a much wider choice of channels and programmes but costs a lot more than terrestrial TV. Cable and satellite have many channels which show certain kinds of programmes, for example Sky Sports, the Movie Channel, and Cartoon Network. Below is a selection of the many channels and programmes you can get on Sky.

Sky News	24-hour
Sky Movies	24-hour
The Disney Channel	6am–10pm
Sky Movies Gold	10pm–6am
Sky Sports 1	7am–varies
Discovery	4pm–2am
UK Living	6am–midnight
MTV	24-hour
VH-1	24-hour
Sky Scottish	6pm–8pm
Sci-Fi Channel	8pm–4am

What Does Television Do for Us?

Television plays a very important part in our lives, as most of us watch a great deal of it. It is perhaps more important than we realise. There are probably four main things it does for us:

Entertain		Educate

Influence		Inform

1. Entertain
Most of us watch television to be entertained. We like to enjoy the programmes we watch and we like to laugh at a comedy, or enjoy a good film or sporting event.

2. Educate
Television also teaches us things, and is a fun way to learn instead of sitting in school all the time. Lots of educational programmes are made especially for children.

3. Influence
Some programmes, and of course adverts, try to persuade us to think a certain way or believe certain things.

4. Inform
Other types of programme are made to keep us up-to-date with what is happening in the world.

ACTIVITY SIX

Below is a list of different types of programme. Try to decide what each type is doing, and fit it into the correct column in the table overleaf. Some may go into more than one column.

Soap, Drama, Film, Snooker, News, Current affairs, Documentary, Comedy, Cookery, Investigative report, Chat show, Business, Cartoon, Football, Weather, Advert, Motoring, Quiz show.

Entertain	Educate	Influence	Inform

How Often do We Watch Television?

Now we know a little bit more about television programmes, we should perhaps look at how often we sit in front of the TV screen, as it obviously has a big effect on our lives. You are going to work out how much time you spend in a normal school day just watching TV. Don't forget to count the time you may watch TV in the morning before you come to school. The table below will help you.

ACTIVITY SEVEN

❶ Copy this table and write down how many hours you watch TV on a normal school day.

Time of day	Number of hours watched
7.00 am–9.00 am	
4.00 pm–6.00 pm	
6.00 pm–8.00 pm	
8.00 pm–10.00 pm	
10.00 pm–12.00 midnight	
	Total hours per day –

❷ Now compare the total you have with your neighbour.

❸ Help your teacher to work out the average for the whole class.

❹ Compare the average for the whole class with your total. Is it higher, lower or the same?

❺ Now write a list of your top ten programmes in your notebook. Give the name of the programme, the type of programme and the channel, e.g.
1. Neighbours – soap – BBC 1.

❻ Write a few sentences about your first choice, saying why you like it best.

Newspapers

Newspapers are certainly a lot older than either radio or television. The first daily newspaper was produced in Britain almost 300 years ago in 1702, although it wasn't really until the 1890s that they became popular. Nowadays, almost every family in the country buys a daily newspaper. Two out of every three adults (66%) read a daily newspaper, and three out of four (75%) read a Sunday newspaper. With a population of around 60 million people in the United Kingdom, that's an awful lot of newspapers!

Types of Newspaper

Newspapers come in two main types – **quality newspapers**, sometimes called broadsheet, and **popular newspapers**, sometimes called tabloids. You can usually tell by simply looking at the newspapers which is which, as broadsheet newspapers are twice the size of tabloid newspapers.

National Daily Newspapers

Many newspapers are printed every day from Monday to Saturday and are often called the **national dailies**. The diagram below shows some of the more well-known national dailies.

THE EXPRESS

The Guardian NEWSPAPER OF THE YEAR

THE TIMES

THE INDEPENDENT

Daily Scottish Mail WEDNESDAY, APRIL 30, 1997 20₁

THE Sun 22p

ACTIVITY EIGHT

❶ Can you say which of these papers are quality and which are popular?

❷ Do you get any of these papers in your house? If so, which ones?

❸ Are there any of these newspapers that you have never had in your house?

Newspaper Circulation

The number of copies a newspaper sells each day is called its **circulation**. Each newspaper company will be trying to sell more and more papers each day. Tabloid papers sell most copies (remember, they are sometimes called popular newspapers). The table below shows the top ten papers in the UK in terms of the number of copies they sell each day:

Newspaper	Average Circulation (1996)
1 SUN	4,057,668
2 MIRROR	2,484,338
3 MAIL	2,049,100
4 EXPRESS	1,257,880
5 TELEGRAPH	1,040,316
6 STAR	668,694
7 TIMES	668,640
8 GUARDIAN	398,661
9 FINANCIAL TIMES	303,573
10 INDEPENDENT	281,588

(Source: adapted from Benn's Media and Willing's Press Guide.)

Scottish Daily Newspapers

In Scotland, we have our own daily newspapers, and although not all of them are owned and printed in Scotland, they each report on Scottish news and mainly carry stories about what is happening in Scotland. The diagram below shows some of the Scottish daily newspapers:

Daily Record

Scotland's Independent Newspaper
EST 1783 GLASGOW **THE HERALD**

NEWSPAPER OF THE YEAR
THE SCOTSMAN

ACTIVITY NINE

❶ Can you say which of these papers are quality and which are popular?

❷ Do you get any of these papers in your house? If so, which ones?

❸ Are there any of these newspapers that you have never had in your house?

Scottish Newspaper Circulation

The table below shows how many papers each of the main dailies sells.

Newspaper	Average Circulation 1996
1 DAILY RECORD	738,544
2 HERALD	106,192
3 SCOTSMAN	76,921

(Source: adapted from Benn's Media and Willing's Press Guide.)

Sunday Newspapers

The daily newspapers only come out on Monday to Saturday, and separate newspapers are printed on a Sunday. Some of them are linked to a daily newspaper, while others are different altogether. The table below shows the best-selling UK Sunday newspapers:

Sunday newspaper	Average Circulation 1996
1 NEWS OF THE WORLD	4,607,189
2 SUNDAY MIRROR	2,425,328
3 MAIL ON SUNDAY	2,114,066
4 PEOPLE	2,064,439
5 SUNDAY TIMES	1,289,887
6 SUNDAY EXPRESS	1,282,654
7 SUNDAY TELEGRAPH	658,103
8 OBSERVER	455,926

(Source: adapted from Benn's Media and Willing's Press Guide.)

Can you say which ones are tabloid and which are broadsheet?

Scotland's Sunday Newspapers

In Scotland, as with the daily newspapers, we find that there are Scottish Sunday newspapers too.

The table below shows how many copies each of the main Scottish Sunday newspapers sells:

Scottish Sunday newspaper	Average Circulation 1996
1 SUNDAY POST	940,349
2 SUNDAY MAIL	884,279
3 SCOTLAND ON SUNDAY	90,916

(Source: adapted from Benn's Media and Willing's Press Guide.)

The diagram below shows the main Scottish Sunday newspapers:

Can you say which of these are tabloid and which are broadsheet?

Other Newspapers

So far, we have been looking mainly at daily and Sunday newspapers, but there are other types of newspaper including evening, weekly, local and free newspapers. See if you can bring one of these types of newspaper into the class and compare them with the daily and Sunday papers.

What's in a Newspaper?

'Newspaper' is not a very good name for these publications, as each of them contains a lot more than just news. If it was only news, we could probably find this out more quickly and more cheaply on the radio and TV. So, why do people read newspapers? The illustrations overleaf show us some of the things that can be found in a newspaper. You could add more of your own.

What Should You Believe?

You should not believe everything you read, just because it's in a newspaper, especially if it's in a popular paper. Newspapers can make mistakes and get their facts wrong. Even worse, they tend to exaggerate or sometimes distort some stories to sell more copies and make more money. Unlike radio and television, newspapers do not have the same restrictions on how they can report the news. In fact, most newspapers will support a particular political party and will try to persuade their readers to do the same. You should remember this when reading anything in a newspaper.

ACTIVITY TEN

❶ Collect a selection of five or six different daily newspapers for the same day. Your whole class can share this task.

❷ Make two lists – 'Popular' and 'Quality'. Put the name of each newspaper into the correct column.

❸ Find FOUR pieces of evidence from any popular newspaper to show that it is not a quality newspaper. Your teacher will help you with this.

❹ Compare the stories in the newspapers. Choose one newspaper and find an example of a) bias and b) exaggeration.

Computers

In the 1960s and 1970s, computers were mostly used by big companies and businesses. Very few people had one at home and if they did, it was probably for playing games on. The 1980s and 1990s have seen an incredible growth in home computer sales, and as they became more popular, prices have fallen so more people could afford one.

ACTIVITY ELEVEN

Do you have a computer at home? If so, write a few sentences describing what it can do and what you use it for. If you don't have one, describe what kind you would like to have.

Computers have only really become part of the media in recent years. The development of things like the Internet, World Wide Web and e-mail have led some people to include them with radio, television and newspapers. Look back at the definition of the media at the start of this chapter. Would you include computers with the others?

The Internet

Many of you may have heard of the Internet, but you may not know exactly what it is. The leaflet below will help to explain it to you.

Get on the Internet with CompuServe

The UK's No.1 connection to the Internet with over 4.5 million members worldwide

Everyone's talking about it. The Internet, the Information Superhighway, cyberspace, the infobahn...there's enough jargon flying around to confuse even the seasoned computer user.

We say, forget all the techno-babble. At **CompuServe**, we've made it incredibly **easy and affordable** to get the most from the exciting new world of online communication, information and entertainment.

Load the enclosed software, and it's easy to join CompuServe for the most comprehensive online service in the world:

- Fast connection to the **Internet** and the **World Wide Web.**
- Your very own Internet **e-mail** address, enabling you to communicate and swap information with over **30 million people** around the globe.
- Access to more than **3,000** exciting and informative CompuServe Services at the mere **click of an icon.**
- All this and more is available via a **local-rate call** from most of the UK!

Just sign up and GO

Signing up couldn't be easier.

All you need to get online is a computer, a modem and the FREE software included in this pack. You will find your software and installation instructions on the enclosed software wallet. Just follow the step-by-step procedures and then the world will be on your computer screen faster than you can say "World Wide Web"!

How to find your way around

Accessing CompuServe Services and the Internet is effortless, because we have adopted an easy-to-use Windows-type approach. To browse any area of interest, simply click on the clearly labelled menu bar or icon.

Internet Browser CompuServe's fast and user-friendly browser software makes it easy to get on the Internet in a few simple steps. Just click on the Internet Browser icon. You can also use your own Internet access software, such as Netscape.

Traffic Light Take a shortcut to the service you want by using what are known as "GO" words. Simply click on the Traffic Light icon and then enter the relevant word. Look out for the Traffic Lights and GO words throughout this guide, shown alongside a selection of CompuServe Services and Web page ("http://") addresses accessible in this way.

Find Use this command to locate the services you need fast. For example, for a list of music-related services, click on the Find icon and enter "MUSIC".

Favourite Places Click on this icon to gain instant access to the services you access most often. You can personalise your own Favourite Places list by storing services you expect to use frequently.

Mail Save money by reading your e-mail offline. Click this icon to retrieve all mail that has arrived for you.

page **3**

Already, computers are to be found in many homes and millions of people are able to communicate with each other quickly and cheaply.

Media Timeline

Look at the Media Timeline below which helps to show the rapid growth of the various methods of communicating over the past 300 years. Copy it and keep the timeline up to date by adding important developments as they happen.

1702 First British newspaper	1895 Radio invented	1896 Daily Mail newspaper	1925 TV invented by Logie Baird	1927 BBC radio broadcast
				1936 BBC TV in London
1977 TV Teletext first set up	1969 Colour TV introduced	1967 BBC 2 started in the UK	1958 ITV set up	1946 BBC TV to all of the UK
1982 Channel 4 set up in the UK				
1983 Breakfast TV started in UK	1985 Cable TV first set up	1989 Satellite TV started in UK	1996 Internet is more popular	1997 Channel 5 started
				1998
			2000	1999

Advertising and the Media

Although the media is mainly concerned with communicating information and news to lots of people, it is also used by companies and people for advertising. Advertising is all around us, and it must work, because companies can sometimes spend millions of pounds advertising their products. They use many different ways to persuade us to buy their product, and a successful advert will remain in your mind long after you have heard or seen it.

ACTIVITY TWELVE

Many adverts have a catchy slogan which makes them stick in our minds. Copy the table below into your notebook and see whether you can think of any you have seen or heard; then put them into the table. The first one has been done for you.

Product	Slogan
Mars bar	A Mars a day helps you work, rest and play.

This is just one of the methods that advertisers use to persuade us to buy their products. The diagram below shows us some of the other things they use.

Glamour

Admiration

Humour

Health and fitness

Part of the crowd

Science and technology

Sex appeal

Fear

ACTIVITY THIRTEEN

Look at the last diagram showing the different methods advertisers use to persuade us to buy their products. In your notebook give an example of each method, e.g. Humour – 'Weetabix' – driving instructor singing 'I will survive'.

Appeal	Product
Glamour	
Admiration	
Humour	
Health and fitness	
Part of the crowd	
Science and technology	
Sex appeal	
Fear	

Cost of Advertising

Advertising is not cheap. The table below shows how much it cost to show a 60-second advert on certain ITV channels in 1996. This figure does not include the cost of making the advert.

Channel	Cost of a 60-second spot in £
Border	7,000
Carlton	90,000
Scottish	36,000
Meridian	70,000
Channel 4	150,000
Ulster	6,000
Anglia	30,000
Central	50,000
Granada	72,000

TV Adverts

On average, each hour on ITV channels will have around 12 minutes' worth of advertising. This is how ITV makes its money. Remember, there is no advertising on BBC1 and BBC2, as they get their money from the TV licence fee.

ACTIVITY FOURTEEN

Watch an ITV channel tonight and choose an hour-long spot, say from 4.00 pm to 5.00 pm or from 7.00 pm to 8.00 pm, and take a note of:

a) How many adverts are shown altogether in this hour?

b) How long in seconds does each advert last?

c) How long in total did adverts last during that hour?

d) What were the different appeals used in those adverts?

Then choose one of the adverts that you particularly liked and write a few sentences about it. (Hint – this might be easier to do if you can record an hour on ITV.)

Newspapers and Advertising

Newspapers also rely on raising money through advertising. The money from sales alone would not be enough to pay for the cost of producing the paper. It also costs a lot of money to advertise in a newspaper. The table below shows the cost of a full-page advert in selected newspapers.

Daily newspaper	Cost of a full-page advert in £* 1996
DAILY MIRROR	25,900
TIMES	17,000
TELEGRAPH	37,500
INDEPENDENT	15,500
HERALD (SCOTLAND)	10,700
DAILY RECORD (SCOTLAND)	10,200
Sunday newspaper	**Cost of a full page advert in £* 1996**
SUNDAY MIRROR	28,500
SUNDAY TIMES	11,000
SUNDAY TELEGRAPH	27,500
INDEPENDENT ON SUNDAY	14,000
SUNDAY MAIL (SCOTLAND)	10,745
SUNDAY POST (SCOTLAND)	9,135

*Cost for a full-page black and white advert. Colour can be more expensive, and in some cases almost twice as much.
(Source: adapted from Benn's Media and Willing's Press Guide.)

ACTIVITY FIFTEEN

Using the figures in the table above for daily *or* Sunday newspapers, draw a bar graph and colour each column differently. Think carefully about the scale.

ACTIVITY SIXTEEN

Choose a daily newspaper from the previous list and work out the following:

a) the total number of pages;

b) the number of pages of advertising – count quarter, half and full pages to find the total;

c) using the table above, work out how much money the paper has made from advertising;

d) look back at the circulation figures on pages 58 and 59 and work out how much the paper made from sales. Multiply the price of the paper by the circulation;

e) which is greater – money from advertising or from sales?

Control of Advertising

Advertising has such an important effect on us, that the Government has brought in certain rules that advertisers must follow. These are called the 'Code of Practice' which advertisers must agree to, and there is an independent body called the Advertising Standards Authority (ASA) which makes sure that these rules are kept. The ASA is responsible for ensuring that the system works in the public interest. Its activities include investigating complaints and conducting research.

Apart from following the rules laid down by the Government, adverts must be:

Accurate		Honest
	ADVERTS	
Decent		Fair

Certain types of advert are not allowed. Cigarettes cannot be advertised on TV, and soon sporting events where cigarettes are advertised will be banned from TV. Do you agree?

Rich World/Poor World – Should It Concern Us?

Rich and Poor Countries

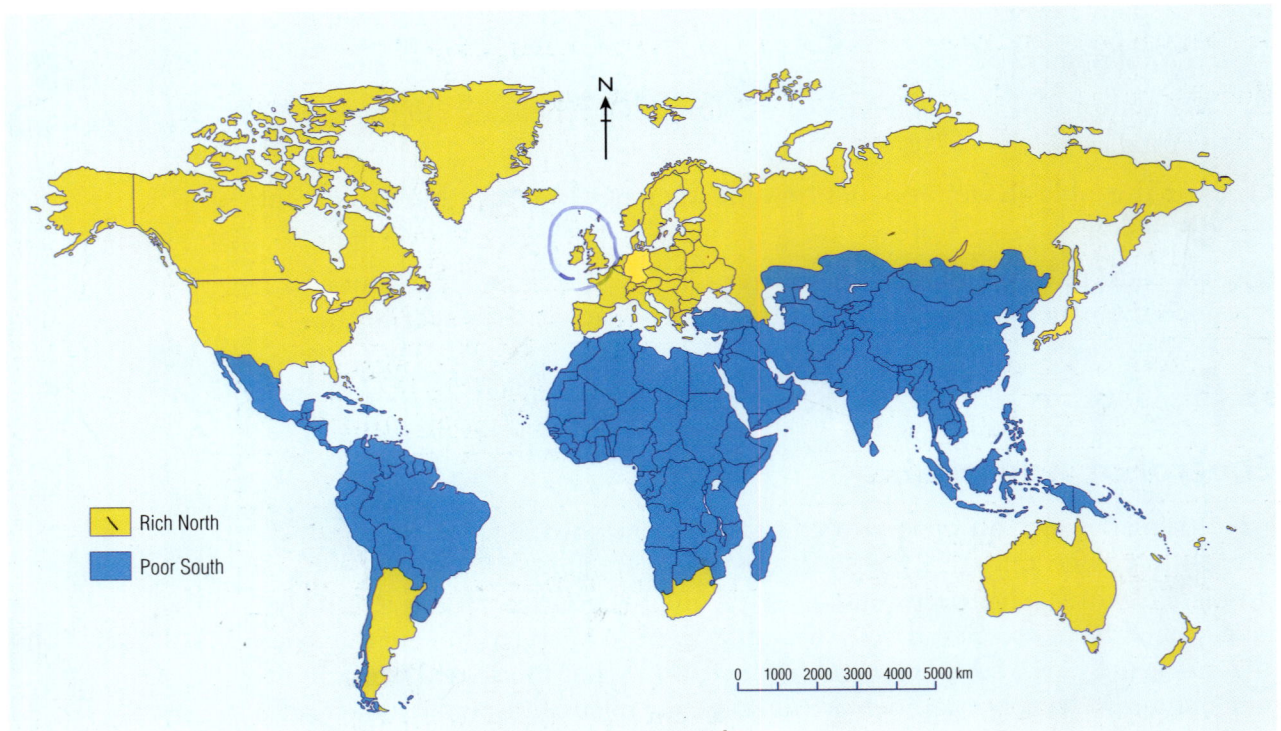

When we look at the way that different people live around the world, we can see that some people are very well off. In our own country, most people have a place to stay, most of them can get all the food they need, and most people do not have to worry about catching diseases from dirty water or bad living conditions.

In other countries, however, we can see on TV and in the newspapers that many people are not so well off. Many people have no homes and have to live in the streets, many people die of starvation or because they do not get the right kinds of food, and many people suffer from illnesses and diseases which can be prevented, like typhoid or cholera.

Those countries which are well off, such as the UK, the USA, Japan, Sweden and Germany, are sometimes called the **developed** countries. It can also be seen, on the map above, that most of these countries are in the **northern half** of the world, and they are often called the **rich north**. Those countries which are not so well off, such as Brazil, Nigeria, Uganda, India and Malaysia, are sometimes called the **developing** countries. It can be seen on the map that they can be found in the **southern half** of the world, and they are often called the **poor south**.

ACTIVITY ONE

Your teacher will give you a blank map of the world and an atlas. Find all the countries listed on Resource Sheet 24 which are the **rich** countries, label them and colour them in using one colour. Then find those countries which are the **poor** countries, label them and colour them in using a different colour. Remember to put a key on your map to show what you have done.

Differences between Rich and Poor Countries

When we compare rich and poor countries, we can see great differences between them. The table below shows what the main differences are.

The north	The south
25% of world population	75% of world population
85% of world industries	15% of world industries
80% of world resources used	20% of world resources used
65% of world grain crops	35% of world grain crops
life expectancy of 75 years	life expectancy of 50 years
one doctor for every 500 people	one doctor for every 7000 people
one car for every 4 people	one car for every 10,000 people

(Adapted from UN sources.)

ACTIVITY TWO

Copy the table above into your notebook, and write a few sentences to explain why you think people in the north are better off than people in the south. You should mention: **food**, **health** and **standard of living**.

How Poor are the Poor Countries?

When we look at the differences between rich and poor countries, there are a number of different ways of seeing just how poor some countries are. The table below shows a list of rich and poor countries all mixed up. It also shows how we can judge how well off some rich countries are compared to the poor countries. The greater the differences between the figures, the greater the differences between the countries.

Life expectancy is the length of time you might be expected to live on average in that country. Infant mortality is the number of babies who die before they reach one year old. GNP is a measure of how rich the country is.

Country	Life expectancy	Birth rate per 1000	Infant mortality per 1000	Daily food intake (cal)	GNP $ (1994)
USA	76	8.7	9.7	3642	25,880
Nigeria	49	46.2	121	2114	280
Sweden	78	13.7	5.8	3049	23,530
UK	76	13.8	9.5	3218	18,340
Japan	79	10.4	4.8	2858	34,630
Brazil	65	27.3	63	2643	2,970
Germany	77	12.1	7.5	3476	25,580
India	58	32	95	2204	320
Malaysia	68	29.5	30	2723	3,480
Uganda	49	52.2	107	2221	190

ACTIVITY THREE

❶ Take each of the headings in turn and explain what the differences mean.

❷ Which countries in the table are the rich countries?

❸ Which countries in the table are the poor countries?

❹ How did you decide which countries were in which list?

World Population

One of the biggest problems facing the poor countries is the fact that they have such a large share of the people in the world. This share is also growing very quickly. The table overleaf shows just what a problem this is.

Country	Population 1990 (millions)	Population 2020 (millions)	Population will double in
Japan (rich)	124	124	–
USA (rich)	251	294	92.4 years
UK (rich)	57	61	301.3 years
Germany (rich)	79	77	–
Nigeria (poor)	119	273	23.6 years
Brazil (poor)	150	234	35.7 years
India (poor)	853	1374	32.7 years
Malaysia (poor)	18	27	27.9 years
Uganda (poor)	18	42	19.5 years

ACTIVITY FOUR

Write a few sentences in your notebook to explain the main differences between the rich and the poor countries in terms of their population growth.

Why So Many People?

Many people in poor countries realise that having such a large growth in your population will cause problems, especially if you are already finding it hard to clothe and feed and house the people at the moment. They find it difficult, however, to bring this population growth under control. There are a number of reasons for the growth in poor countries' populations:

Poor education Standards in education are poor in many countries, and women in particular are not educated in methods of family planning.	**High infant mortality** Many children may die at an early age, so families might tend to have more children to make sure some of them survive.
Poor status of women Women are generally not involved in making decisions in many poor countries, and are seen as being there only to bring up the children.	**Farming communities** In many poor countries the main jobs people have are on farms. The bigger the family, the more workers.
Family planning In rural areas especially, people do not have access to proper methods of family planning and cannot control the size of their families.	**Old age** There are few places in poor countries where the elderly can get a pension. The more children you have, the more there are to look after you.

ACTIVITY FIVE

❶ What could be done to improve the chances of being able to control the size of families?

❷ What could be done to improve the chances of children surviving in greater numbers?

❸ How might more elderly people be helped to survive without relying on their children?

China's Solution to the Problem

China has a population of over 1200 million people, and this is increasing by over 30,000 every day. The Government decided that it had to take drastic measures to try to bring this population explosion under control. It introduced a law, which said that Chinese couples were only allowed to have one child. If a couple has more than one child, they can be fined or have their electricity cut off. There is great pressure on women to have abortions, and many female babies have been killed at birth, as males are considered to be better.

ACTIVITY SIX

❶ Is it right for the Government in China to limit the size of families?

❷ Why do you think so many female babies are killed?

❸ Can you think of any other means the Government could use to keep population growth down? Discuss this in small groups and report to your teacher.

The Food Problem

There is enough food in the world to feed everybody, but it is not equally distributed. People in northern countries have more food than they need, and they tend to suffer from illnesses and diseases that are linked to over-eating, like heart disease. In the south, millions of people are starving. Whether you have enough food depends on how poor you are. People in the UK consume 125% of their calorie needs, while people in Ethiopia have just 71%. Although there is on average enough food for everyone in Malawi, people there have to spend 55% of their income to buy it.

Very few people who die as a result of food shortages, actually die of starvation. They either die from illnesses brought on by malnutrition (not getting enough of the right kinds of food), or they die because of diseases from contaminated water, which their weakened bodies cannot fight off.

Coffee picking in Kenya

ACTIVITY SEVEN

❶ Can you list five different types of food that we get from Africa.

❷ Why is it important to eat the right kinds of food?

❸ Can you think of any disease you might get from contaminated water?

❹ Collect the labels from any foodstuffs from Africa that you have in the house.

Famine in Africa

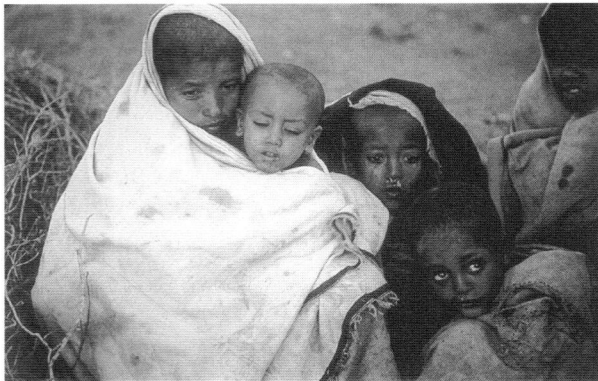

We often hear on the news that there is a famine going on in Africa. Sometimes it seems that famine never ends. Not all countries that have droughts and food shortages end up having famines. There are a number of different reasons for famines:

Geography	Some places have better climates, soils and conditions.
Food prices	Poor people cannot afford to buy what food there is.
Civil war	Wars make it difficult to guarantee that food can be grown.
Cash crops	Much of what is grown is sold abroad to make money.
Poverty	Ordinary people cannot always look after themselves.

ACTIVITY EIGHT

❶ Which parts of Africa might not be suitable for growing food?

❷ Why do wars make it hard for poor countries?

❸ What would you do to help an area of famine?

How Can We Help Poor Countries?

When you see the big differences that sometimes exist between rich and poor countries, you might think that people in the rich countries should be doing something to help people in the poor countries. In fact, there are lots of examples of help, or **aid**, that is given to poor countries. The diagrams on the following page show where aid comes from and what the main types of aid are.

Sources of Aid

OXFAM
UNITED KINGDOM AND IRELAND

Christian Aid
AN OFFICIAL AGENCY OF BRITISH AND IRISH CHURCHES

Governments	Organisations	Voluntary
The governments of rich countries like the UK and the USA will often send help to the governments of poor countries.	Groups of countries which have joined together in organisations like the United Nations will send help to poor countries.	Voluntary organisations, like Oxfam and Christian Aid, which get money from ordinary people will help people in poor countries.

Types of Aid

Financial aid (money)	Food aid	Emergency aid
Many rich countries give **loans** to poor countries, but they have to pay even more back, as interest is added on. **Grants** can also be given, which do not need to be paid back.	Rich countries sometimes have a lot more food than they need, and they can send things like wheat, corn, flour, powdered milk and cheese to people in poor countries.	Sometimes we hear of disasters like earthquakes, floods and droughts in poor countries, and rich countries help by sending things like tents, food and clothing, and medicines.
Experts	**Machinery**	**Military aid**
Rich countries can often send out experts and volunteers like doctors, teachers, engineers and managers to help poor countries build up their own businesses and industries and help ordinary people.	Special farming machinery like tractors and harvesters can be sent to poor countries, and machinery for use in factories can also be sent to build up industries.	If a friendly government is under attack from rebels, rich countries can help it by sending tanks, guns, and sometimes troops to help it stay in power.

ACTIVITY NINE

Take each of the types of aid listed in the boxes on the previous page and say whether you think it is more likely to benefit the Government of that country or the ordinary people. Give reasons for your answers.

How does Britain Help Poor Countries?

Spraying a pineapple crop, Kenya

The British Government and the people of Britain help poor countries in a number of different ways:

Bilateral aid

This is when the British Government gives help directly to another country. Sometimes this help is called **tied aid**. This means that the money given by Britain has to be spent on British goods. For example, Kenya is given money to buy British tractors.

Multilateral aid

This is when Britain gives money to organisations which help poor countries. The three most important organisations are the United Nations, the World Bank and the European Union. These organisations decide where the goods will be bought from.

Voluntary aid

Individual people often give contributions to voluntary groups who help people in the developing countries. Some examples of these groups are the Save the Children Fund, Oxfam, Comic Relief, Christian Aid, and Blue Peter.

OXFAM
UNITED KINGDOM AND IRELAND

Christian Aid
AN OFFICIAL AGENCY OF BRITISH AND IRISH CHURCHES

ACTIVITY TEN

❶ Why do you think the British Government likes some aid to be tied aid?

❷ Why do some of the aid organisations like to decide how to spend the aid?

❸ What kinds of thing do the voluntary groups do to raise money?

❹ Can you think of any recent examples?

The United Nations Agencies

The United Nations was set up in 1945 to try to keep the peace between countries and to help improve the living standards of people around the world. In order to try to achieve this, the United Nations has created a number of specialised agencies. Some of these agencies are directly involved in the poor countries of the world and have given lots of help there. You may have seen some examples of the work they do on television.

1 **The World Health Organisation (WHO)**
   This agency tries to help people with their medical problems. Many countries in the south cannot afford a National Health Service, and are not able to give free health care to their people. WHO helps these countries organise their health services. They help to train doctors and nurses, and to carry out mass vaccination programmes. They also try to wipe out diseases like smallpox and leprosy. In emergencies they rush to help stop epidemics like typhus.

2 Food and Agriculture Organisation (FAO)
The FAO tries to fight against hunger throughout the world by helping to train people in the latest farming, fishing and forestry methods. It tries to introduce the latest technology to make farming easier. It also provides emergency aid when there is a disaster like a famine, a drought or an earthquake.

3 United Nations International Children's Emergency Fund (UNICEF)
This agency tries to help improve conditions for children in the world. It aims to help improve children's health, food and education. There are millions of children around the world who don't have the basic necessities of life, and UNICEF tries to help them. They organise emergency relief for children after a disaster. They run many school projects to lower the illiteracy rates in many countries.

4 United Nations Educational, Scientific and Cultural Organisation (UNESCO)
This agency is concerned with improving all the different aspects of education. It sets up science and technology centres. It sends teachers to help improve basic levels of reading and writing. It tries to develop the arts and culture of different countries.

If you would like more information on the UN agencies, look at pages 105–107.

ACTIVITY ELEVEN

❶ Copy the table below into your notebook and put the correct project into the correct column:

Agency	Project
WHO	
FAO	
UNICEF	
UNESCO	

a) a new school in Egypt

b) a history museum in Uganda

c) a farming college in the Sudan

d) a hospital in Somalia.

How Well off are We?

Quite often we hear people in this country say that they have no money, they can't buy anything, they can't go anywhere and they are living in poverty. If we compare our lives to that of some people living in developing countries, we might find out that we are not really that bad after all. Read the true story below of women working in different parts of the developing world, and answer the questions which follow:

All for Buttons

Selina, who makes shirts in Dhaka (you may be wearing one) does make money from her job, writes Jane Scott. To be precise, she makes £6 a month after paying for food, shelter and transport, but this usually goes on health bills; sitting over a sewing machine for 12 hours a day breathing in dust from the cloth causes back strain and the sweetly-named bisinosis, a chronic respiratory problem common to textile workers. That's not counting urinary tract infections (workers are often banned from taking toilet breaks), eye disorders, and the fact that if the factory went up in flames you'd be lucky to find a fire exit. Goodness, veal calves have nothing on this. But then people are prepared to die for veal calves.

The journey your shirt has made from the bale to your back may interest you. It could have been cut out in Hong Kong, sent to an Indonesian workshop for making up, shipped to West Yorkshire, and placed with out-workers who sew on buttons. Then the retailer can slap on a 'Made in Britain' label and mislead you, the consumer, into buying it in good faith. Some 70% of textile workers are women, and it is their stories Oxfam is telling in a campaign launched this week to pressure main street retailers into improving working conditions.

Because the last thing to do is stop buying the clothes. When a US Bill was proposed to prohibit the import of goods made with child labour, Bangladeshi factory owners promptly threw 40,000 child workers out on the streets to avoid a crippling boycott.

It's a complicated business, intervening in a poorer nation's economy. The Bangladeshi textile industry has grown from nothing, 15 years ago, to providing two-thirds of the country's export earnings today. If the industry could provide labour so cheaply it is because there was huge poverty and unemployment and women, as the working majority, have benefited. It is now acceptable for women to travel to the cities to find work, they have increased social status and bargaining power, and the average age of marriage has risen.

The Third World, says Oxfam, needs to keep on making clothes. But we should insist that the people who make them have decent wages and working conditions. The lives of textile workers are brutish. Valeska, from Chile, sewed buttons on 2000 garments a week. If the machine broke, she didn't get paid. She never got a contract, because then they could pay below the minimum wage. Estela, from the Dominican Republic, was sacked from one factory after a few days' illness. In another she had to sew up 72 pieces an hour.

Oxfam is asking consumers to hand in ready-printed coupons to major retailers asking whether they have a code of conduct protecting clothing workers. The charity is also lobbying for an international agreement on minimum rights. Because otherwise there'll always be a factory somewhere prepared to undercut the competition – and taking the shirt off someone's back to do it.

(Source: The *Herald*, 20.5.96.)

ACTIVITY TWELVE

Read the article on page 79.

❶ What kind of job does Selina have making shirts in Dhaka?

❷ What's interesting about how this shirt gets to you in the shop?

❸ What happened when the US tried to ban shirts made by child labour in Bangladesh?

❹ What kind of working conditions did Valeska from Chile and Estela from the Dominican Republic have?

❺ How is the charity Oxfam trying to protect clothing workers?

❻ Compare the working conditions of these workers with someone you know who has a job in this country.

❼ Are there laws in this country which would prevent some of the working conditions described in the article being used here?

USA, Land of Opportunity – Is It?

6

What is the Country Like?

The United States of America, to give it its full title, is a country that you probably think you know a great deal about. We see much about it on our television screens. We watch a lot of films that are made there. We even copy many of the styles that start out in America. Ask around your class and see how many people have clothes with the name of a well-known American company or sports team on them. What we see on our television programmes, though, may not be what it is actually like in America. We are going to look at the USA and find out if it is the land of opportunity.

The USA is about 3000 miles from the west coast to the east coast, and about 1500 miles from the northern border to the south. It is a very big country. The climate in the USA varies a lot from one part to another. In the northern states like Minnesota, Wisconsin and Michigan, it can be very cold in winter. In the southern states like Texas and Florida, and western states like California, it can be very hot and humid almost all the year round.

ACTIVITY ONE

Look at the map of the USA on page 81 and see whether you can find and write down the following in your notebooks:

a) Four states beginning with the letter A, eight states beginning with the letter M, four states beginning with the word 'New', two pairs of North and South states.

b) Which states are the following cities in: New York, Los Angeles, Chicago, Miami, San Francisco, Washington DC, and Dallas?

c) Which two states are apart from all the others?

Why did People Go There?

For hundreds of years, America has attracted people from all over the world to come and live there. Many of these people were trying to escape from problems in their own countries, like poverty, wars, or bad governments. They thought that if they came to America, they would be able to solve a lot of their problems. America was seen as the 'land of their dreams'. They felt they were going to the 'American Dream'. There were a number of reasons why they felt this way:

a) there was plenty of land and space to move to;

b) there were lots of opportunities to get work;

c) there was a chance to make a fresh start;

d) there were a lot of freedoms guaranteed for the people, like education, voting and freedom of speech;

e) there were many chances to start up your own business.

ACTIVITY TWO

❶ Why would availability of land encourage many people to go to the USA all those years ago?

❷ Why might it be important for some people to have all the freedoms above?

❸ Why would some people want to start up their own business?

The People of the USA

As a result of all these people coming to America in the past, the USA today is made up of many different groups. The table below shows who the main groups are and how many of them there are in America today.

Group	Number (million)	Percentage
Whites	200	75%
Blacks	30	11%
Hispanics	22	9%
Asians	7	3%
Native Americans	2	1%

Who are These Groups?

Whites –   Most whites are the descendants of immigrants who came from Europe to the USA many years ago. Although they have English, German, Dutch, Italian or Polish surnames, they mix well together and many of them would see themselves just as Americans.

Blacks –   The blacks or African-Americans can trace their ancestors back to Africa and the slave trade. Their colour makes them stand out, and many of them feel that they have not been allowed to share in the American Dream. Many of them live in the large cities in areas called 'ghettoes'.

Hispanics –   These are people who speak Spanish as their first language. They come from Spanish-speaking countries close to America, like Mexico, Puerto Rico, Cuba, and Central and South America, and tend to stick together when they come to the USA.

Asians –   Chinese- and Japanese-Americans have been living in the USA for over 100 years, but they have been joined recently by people from Korea, Vietnam and the Philippines. Many of them tend to be quite well off, and their children generally get a good education.

Native Americans –   These are the descendants of the Indian tribes, like the Sioux and the Cheyenne, and about half of them still live on or near the reservations set up for them by the Government. They are among the poorest groups of people in America.

ACTIVITY THREE

See whether you can list any famous people from the past or the present who belong to each of the five groups of Americans on page 83. Try to get at least three for each group.

America and Democracy

Many of the freedoms which attracted people to America are still important today. In particular, Americans are very concerned to make sure that they have a say in all the decisions taken by the Government which affect their lives. In America there are really three levels of government.

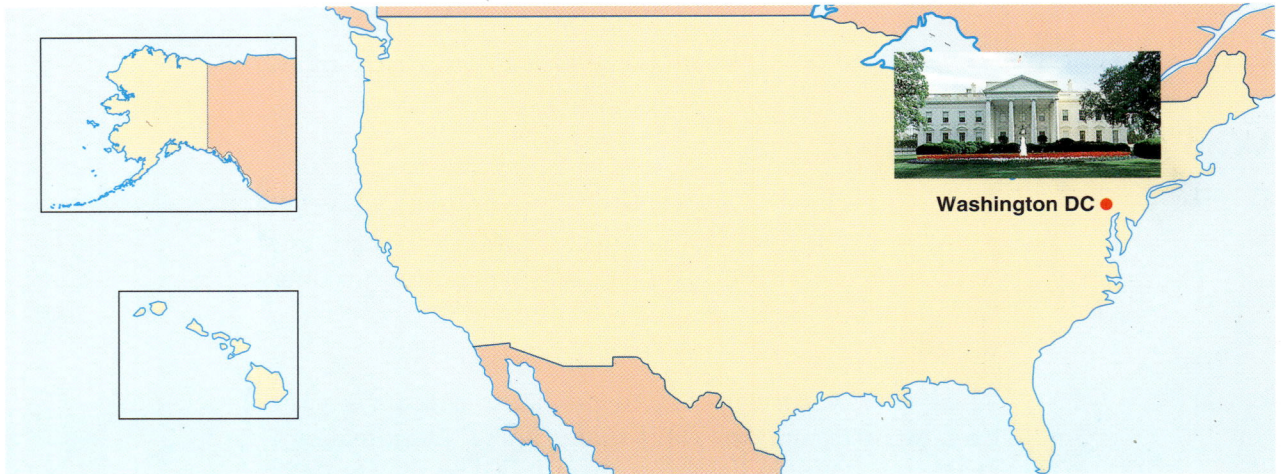

Washington DC

The Federal Government

Bill Clinton, President

The Capitol (Congress building) in Washington DC

The Federal or National Government looks after the interests of all Americans and deals with things like defence and foreign policy. It acts for all of the 'United States' of America. The head of this Federal level of government is the President, and he is elected every four years by the people. He speaks for all Americans, and deals with other world leaders.

Americans also elect representatives to an assembly called Congress. It has two houses or chambers. One is called the Senate and it has 100 Senators, two for each of the 50 states. The other is called the House of Representatives and it has 435 members.

The people elected to this House are sent there on the basis of an area's population. A heavily-populated state like California, which has about 50 million people in it, will have a lot of members elected to the House, whereas a state with a small population like Nevada will only have a few.

ACTIVITY FOUR

❶ Can you think of any other Presidents of America before Bill Clinton?

❷ Give an example of something the President can do on behalf of America.

❸ Can you think of any reason why the Senate has two Senators for each state?

❹ Why does the House of Representatives allocate seats on the basis of population?

❺ How many elected posts at the Federal level do Americans vote for?

The State Governments

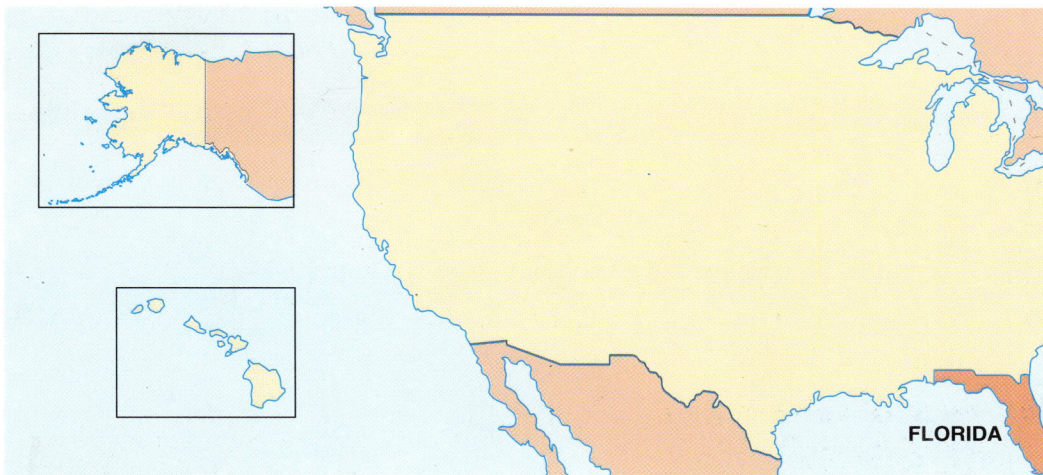

FLORIDA

Each of the 50 states has its own government, like the state of Florida on the map. Some of you may have been there or know someone who has. The person elected to run the state, to do the same kind of job that the President does for the whole of America, is called the Governor. Each state also elects its own Congress, with two houses, called the State Senate and the State House of Representatives. The State Government can pass laws on matters that only affect the people of that state. They may pass laws on education, law and order, and housing. The state police are only allowed to act in their own states and don't have any powers in other states.

ACTIVITY FIVE

❶ Why does America allow each of the 50 states to pass its own laws?

❷ Can you think of any problems this might cause?

❸ How many elected posts at state level do Americans vote for?

City or County Government

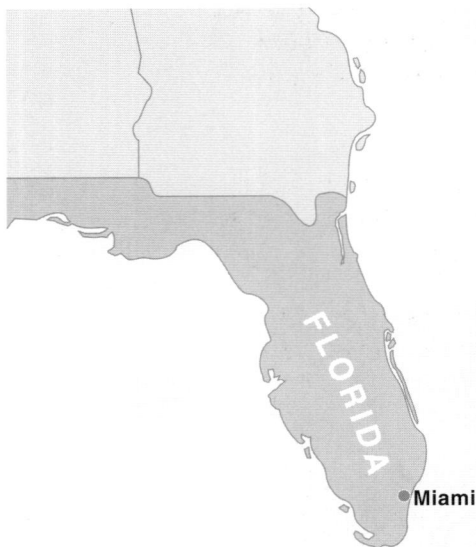

Although each of the states has its own government, these states still have a lot of people in them or cover a large area. The states are divided into smaller areas called counties. The large cities, like Miami, have their own areas. Americans get to vote for a lot of the people who run these smaller areas in each of the states. Perhaps the most important post is that of the mayor. If you've seen 'Batman', you'll know that the man who runs Gotham City is the mayor.

There is also usually a city or a town council to be elected. The local police chief is elected, the judges are elected, schools are run by elected school boards, and many other posts like the fire chief, the chief librarian and the DA or district attorney are chosen by the people. As we said earlier, Americans want to have a say in choosing the people who make decisions which are going to affect their lives.

ACTIVITY SIX

❶ How many elected posts have you been able to count over the three levels of government?

❷ Do you think Americans have too many posts to vote for?

❸ Is it a good idea to vote for people like the police chief, the fire chief and the librarian?

❹ What do you think might happen at elections in America if there are so many posts to vote for?

❺ Try to find information in your school library or local library about elections in America.

What's It Like to Visit America?

America has many attractions for visitors, but Florida is a top choice of travellers from around the world. The climate gives it holiday weather almost all the year round. The table below shows average temperatures in the Orlando area in Fahrenheit.

Month	°F	Month	°F	Month	°F
Jan	72	May	88	Sept	90
Feb	73	Jun	91	Oct	84
Mar	78	Jul	92	Nov	78
Apr	84	Aug	92	Dec	73

The area really took off in 1971 with the opening of Walt Disney World™ and it has grown non-stop ever since. The area also offers golf on nearly 100 excellent courses. There is tennis, waterskiing, horseback riding, and many other outdoor activities. What most visitors go to see, however, are the theme parks. Below are just some of the attractions Florida has to offer.

Walt Disney's Magic Kingdom – Cinderella's Castle is surrounded by seven different Theme-lands that offer fantasy, fun and adventure, with nearly 50 attractions and dozens of shops and restaurants.

Walt Disney's Epcot Centre – This takes you on incredible journeys through time and space at Future World, and there are exotic continents at World Showcase.

Disney MGM Studios – At Hollywood Adventures you can see movies and TV shows actually being made and meet some of the big-name TV stars in person.

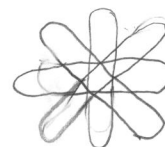

Sea World of Florida – Through more than 20 spectacular attractions like Shamu the killer whale you can enjoy a blend of fun, education and excitement.

To get any closer, you'd need gills.

Universal Studios Florida® – This has over 40 rides, shows and movie set streets, including 'Jaws', 'ET', 'Earthquake' and 'Back to the Future', where everything you saw in the movies can now happen to you.

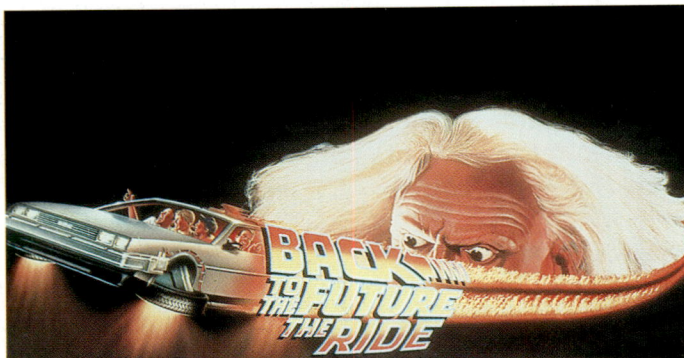

Kennedy Space Center – Take a tour for a close-up view of the Space Shuttle launch pads and see how America got into space.

ACTIVITY SEVEN

❶ Look at the attractions available to visit in Florida and choose the two you would most like to see; give reasons for your choice.

❷ Take a visit to your local travel agent and try to collect some brochures on America. Use them to plan an imaginary holiday for your family.

What's It Like Living in America?

The Typical American?

When Americans show Scotland and Scots people on TV or films, they quite often show us as people who wear kilts, play the bagpipes, eat haggis all the time and talk with funny accents. Is this what we are really like? In the same way, we probably have a good idea of what a typical American looks like?

We have to be careful that we don't look at one small part of America and think that's what all Americans look like and that is how all Americans live. We are going to look at the lives of some Americans to see if they find America is the 'Land of Opportunity', but always remember, America is a vast country with lots of different people, who live many different lifestyles.

Housing

Where you live in America depends very much on your racial background or income. More and more in America, people are going to stay in neighbourhoods where they will find people from their own racial group. In a large American city, for example, you will find areas where nearly all of the people are black, and areas where there are a lot of Hispanics. Many of these areas will be poor areas. There will also be poor areas where most of the people are white.

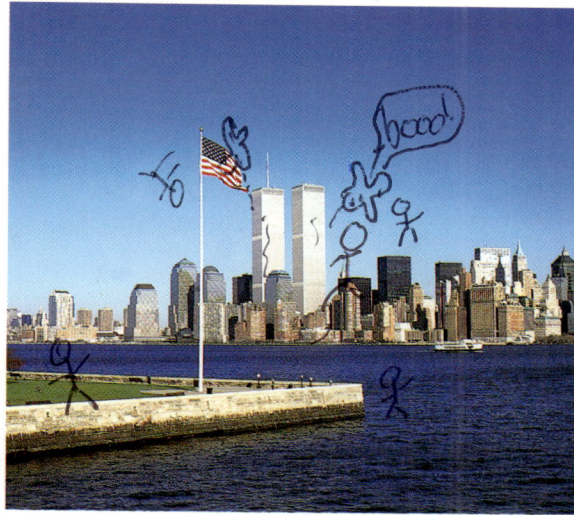

Well-off whites may live in comfortable apartment blocks with security entrances and their own porter. In many cases, whites have moved right out of the city into quite well-off suburbs. Some whites even live in private estates, where they are fenced off from the outside world and have private police to patrol the area. A smaller number of blacks and Hispanics have been able to move into these areas.

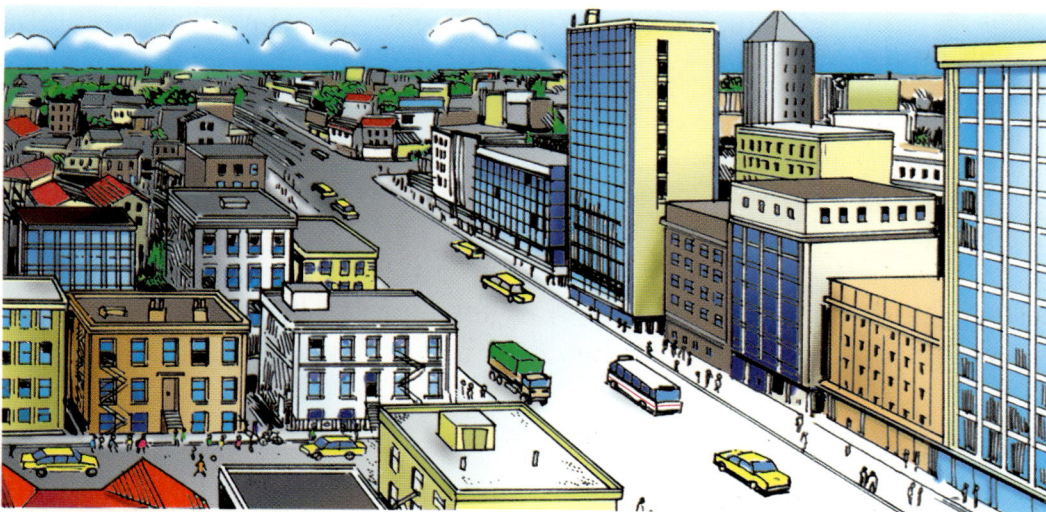

ACTIVITY EIGHT

❶ Why do you think people in America live beside people from their own race?

❷ Why do most blacks and Hispanics seem to live in the poorer parts of the city?

❸ What do you think might happen if more blacks tried to move into white areas?

❹ Would you like to live in a fenced-off estate with gates and security guards? Give reasons for your answer.

Living in Los Angeles

The image we have of living in Los Angeles is probably what we see in the movies and on TV programmes about LA. The story below, however, tells us what it is really like to live in this huge metropolis. Read the story and answer the questions in your notebook.

LA Law and Disorder

Los Angeles, which was 75% white in 1970, will be just 40% white by the year 2000. The USA, and in particular Los Angeles, is finally waking up to the fact that the world has finite resources and the optimism of the '50s and '60s, with the idea of endless growth, is finished, just as surely as the endless summer of gilded white youth on the beaches is finished.

The American Dream – LA style – of owning a home with a yard, has been replaced by the reality of life in tightly guarded condos. There is more than a sneaking suspicion that those who already have their slice of the American pie are not so keen on letting others even sit at the table. It is the most divided city in the world. The racial barriers are high, but the class barriers are absolute. The LA the world knows – beaches, outdoor restaurants, beautiful people – the LA familiar from a hundred movies and TV shows, is actually only West Los Angeles, a semi-circle of privilege bounded by the coast, the Hollywood hills to the north, the airport to the south.

No one I knew ever considered a visit to black South-Central LA or the vast expanse of Latino East LA. It was another world, unknown, unknowable, terrifying. During the filming I was dropping some kids off in Watts. As I drew up at each corner, the looks were not of hatred but of astonishment. This segregation is as absolute as any enforced by South African pass laws. It is so absolute that many of the young Latinos we met have never had any form of conversation with someone of a different race.

(Source: the *Herald*, Jan. 1994 – Alan Clements)

ACTIVITY NINE

❶ What evidence is there that the population of the city of LA is changing?

❷ What are well-off people in the city doing as a result of these changes?

❸ Which part of LA has a lot of these wealthy people?

❹ What evidence is there that blacks and Latinos don't often come into contact with whites?

❺ Would you like to live in LA and, if so, which part would you live in?

Education

The type of school you go to often depends on where you live. This photo shows the glossy image you might see on television. The reality is that schools in the inner cities are often not nice places to be. Read the article below about one school in Los Angeles and answer the questions which follow it.

Where School is a Fortress of Learning

(Adapted from *The Sunday Times*, 23.1.94.)

An 8ft high wire fence surrounds the school premises. Police officers circulate among the pupils at break times. School staff are placed at strategic points with walkie-talkies and have call signs to cover every eventuality. This is Belmont High School in a central district of Los Angeles that has a reputation for gang fights, drug-dealing and violence.

Earthquakes such as the one that devastated parts of the city last week are merely one of the many hazards that children in the area face.

Official US Government figures suggest one in five high school students carries a firearm, knife or club on a regular basis. There are about 3 million thefts and violent crimes on or near school campuses each year – a rate of one every six seconds. It is a problem that is more evident in the inner cities. The Los Angeles Unified School District even has its own police force. With 500 full- or part-time officers, the school police department is responsible for ensuring the safety of 800,000 students and staff as well as property. Every high school has an armed police presence at all times, and police cars patrol school sites day and night.

Inside Belmont High, staff pride themselves on a tough but fair approach to discipline. No weapons are allowed on site: signs on the school walls make the point. There are even random checks to ensure the rule is obeyed. Students must be in class on time. If they are not, they are sent to a 'tardy room', supervised by staff. If their lateness persists they are expelled. As if to underline the point, the theme music from 'Jaws' is sometimes played to warn students when lessons are about to start.

Arthur Darden, the police officer stationed full-time at Belmont High, sees the school as a haven. 'This is one of the highest crime areas in Los Angeles, but the school is a safe place. Discipline is good and we are protecting the kids in the school from their own neighbourhood, not from each other.' Outside, drive-by shootings, drugs and related crimes are everyday events in the surrounding communities. Inside, there are playing fields, an auditorium and student shop alongside the three-storey school buildings. Mitchell, the police chief, sums up his optimism about the area. 'The egg can be boiled from the inside out. The changes that we will see in our schools can spread outwards to the local community. Our schools can help to make our society better. That way we have a future.'

91

❶ What precautions are taken in Belmont High School to prevent trouble?

❷ What examples are given of crime levels in America's schools?

❸ What do the authorities do to prevent crime in Belmont High?

❹ Why does the school's police officer think of the school as a haven?

❺ How does this school compare to your own school?

Poverty in America

The American Dream that attracted so many people to the country in the past, has always been what Americans expect to have a chance of achieving. Success at school should mean success at your job, and should give all Americans an equal chance to get a good standard of living. Some Americans do achieve this ideal and live in a nice house, in a nice area, and have lots of money to spend on the things that make living in America so enjoyable and exciting. In the past few years, however, the gap between rich and poor has been getting wider, and there are an increasing number of people who are finding it harder and harder to make ends meet. The table below shows the number of people living in poverty in 1990, the number of people unemployed, and average family income.

Number of people living in poverty (Source: US Census, 1991)

Ethnic group	1990
White	9%
Black	31%
Hispanic	28%

Unemployment rates by ethnic groups (Source: US Census, 1991)

Ethnic group	1990
White	6%
Black	12%
Hispanic	10%

Average family income (Source: US Census, 1991)

Ethnic group	1990
White	$27,000
Black	$17,000
Hispanic	$20,000

ACTIVITY ELEVEN

❶ Draw three bar charts in your notebook to show (1) the number of people living in poverty, (2) the number of people unemployed, and (3) average family income.

❷ Write a few sentences to explain what the bar charts are telling you.

What Help do the Poor Get?

Americans often use the word 'welfare' to mean the types of help that they get from the Government. Some of this help comes in the form of cash, and some in the form of services to try and help people on low incomes. These are aimed at helping the poor to meet their basic needs – food, clothing, health care and shelter. The table below shows some of the different ways the Government helps the poor.

The American Welfare System

Name	Purpose
Social Security	Pays for state pensions for the elderly
Unemployment insurance	Pays money to people who are out of work
Medicare	Pays for the medical bills of elderly people
Medicaid	Pays for the medical bills of the poor
Aid to families with dependent children (AFDC)	Pays for help to single parents with children
School lunch programme	Pays for free or cheap meals for poor children
Food stamps	Pays for food for poor families
Public housing	Pays for houses built for the less well off

ACTIVITY TWELVE

❶ Why does the Government seem to help poor people out in a lot of different ways?

❷ Choose three of the types of help above and explain why you think poor people need them.

❸ What do you think would happen if the Government did not help out?

Crime in America

In recent years there has been a huge increase in the number of crimes being committed in the USA. Many people believe it is linked to the poorer social and economic conditions that are to be found, particularly in the areas dominated by the ethnic minorities. What has been more worrying, however, for most Americans, is that a lot of this increase in crime is beginning to be seen in areas outside the inner cities. The tables below show some facts and figures about crime in the USA.

Murder rate (Source: US Census, 1990)

Country	Rate per million people 1990
USA	95
Britain	5

Arrests of juveniles in USA (Source: New Internationalist, August 1996)

Ethnic group	Increase 87/88
White	1%
Non-whites	42%

Prison rate in USA (Source: New Internationalist, August 1996)

Ethnic group	Number per 100,000 (1991)
White males	352
Black males (age 25–29)	6301

ACTIVITY THIRTEEN

❶ What does the first part of the table tell you about violent crime in Britain compared to America?

❷ Explain what the second part of the table is telling you about which groups seem to be more involved in crime.

❸ How much more likely are young black men to go to prison compared to white men?

❹ What impression do you get about crime in the USA from the table?

USA, Land of Opportunity – Is It?

When people first started to come to the USA many years ago, the country was seen as one which welcomed them with open arms. The freedoms, the land, the opportunities, all attracted people from almost every part of the globe. Today, with all the problems America has, there may not be such a warm welcome for new immigrants.

Many people still come to the USA looking for a new life, and many of them enter the country illegally. It has been estimated that during the early 1990s, illegal immigrants were entering the country at a rate of 500,000 each year. Most of these immigrants have made for California, the 'Golden State', where they see themselves being able to take part in this 'American Dream'.

Going to America?

Despite its many problems of crime, poverty and tension among its racial groups, the USA remains for millions of people a very attractive country. The USA is, after all, the richest and most powerful country in the world and it has great influence on what happens in the rest of the world.

Probably every nationality in the world is represented in the population of the USA and the country has been home to millions of immigrants for the past two hundred years. Millions more would like to settle in the USA because, despite its problems, it can still offer a better and safer environment than many people have in their own country.

The USA and the UK have been close friends for a long time and have much in common. In the past, many people went to live in America from the UK, and most Americans speak the same language as us. Things are not quite the same, however.

ACTIVITY FOURTEEN

❶ What do Americans call the following:

| Pavement | Petrol | Chemist Shop | Trousers | Water Tap |
| Car Boot | Car Bumper | Biscuits | Nappies | Chips |

❷ Name ten American companies which are well-known in the UK, e.g. Ford.

❸ Name three American fast-food companies which are popular in the UK.

❹ Name three American sports which are popular in the UK.

❺ Do you agree with the view that the UK and the USA have much in common? Find some evidence to support your view.

❻ Are there any things in the USA that you would not like to see coming here?

The American Dream

For millions of 'ordinary' American families, the USA is the best country in the world and they are proud to live there. One of the things which keeps attracting people to the USA and which keeps people living there, is the idea of the 'American Dream'. This is the idea that if you work hard you can make a success of your life. It doesn't matter who you are or where you come from, you should be able to take the opportunities that are offered to you. That is why the USA is sometimes called the Land of Opportunity. Many Americans also place a great deal of importance on the rights and freedoms they are allowed in the USA. As we saw earlier, the USA is a Democracy and this means individual people have rights and freedoms which are guaranteed.

Look at what these Americans have to say about their country:

Austin Hamilton (47) Black	**Casey Kelso (13) White**
Sure the USA has got its problems, what country ain't. What about you in England? Ain't you got crime? I read last week about old ladies getting mugged in the street and about your problems with drugs. So don't give me any c**p about the good old USA being a violent country. Listen fella, I think you're just plain jealous 'cos you don't live here and you can't do all the things we can.	There are too many bad things written about the USA by people who have never lived here. Yes, there is crime and violence and poverty and drugs, but every country has these nowadays. If you get a good education and work hard, you can really become somebody. Me? I want to be the first female President of the USA and my mum says I can make it if I really want it.
Mandy Kim (17) Asian	**Oscar Ramirez (22) Hispanic**
My mum and dad came from Korea with nothing and worked hard to get where they are now. My dad runs a small business and works long hours to keep it going. I was born here and my parents want me to go to college to become a doctor. Back in Korea, they would never have been able to do that.	I arrived in America with my parents from Mexico when I was only 8. At first when I went to school I found it hard because I couldn't speak any English. I worked hard at school and now I have a job as an electrician. I'm married and I own my house and someday I'll have my own business.

ACTIVITY FIFTEEN

❶ Write down what you think the phrase 'American Dream' means.

❷ Do you think that the USA is a 'Land of Opportunity'?

❸ Look back to the section on Decisions – Who Makes Them (page 12). Make a list of the rights and freedoms that Amerian citizens have which we also have in Britain. Can you think of any others you could add to that list for the USA? (Think about the right to protect yourself, for example.)

❹ Read the views of the four people above. What evidence is there to show that they believe the USA is a Land of Opportunity?

❺ Write a short article similar to these four examples, but from the point of view of someone who might not see life in the USA as being so good.

❻ Make a list of ten TV programmes which are made in the USA and which are popular here (e.g. 'Friends' or 'The Simpsons').

Try to find an example of the following from these programmes: wealth; poverty; crime; rights; Blacks; Hispanics; Asians; The American Dream; Immigration.

❼ Do you think the programmes you have chosen show the USA in a good or a bad light?

❽ Would you like to live in the USA? Give reasons for your answer.

7 International Problems – Can We Solve Them?

Introduction

Can you remember the story of Robinson Crusoe, when he was alone on his island, and he had to do everything for himself? This made life very difficult for him, and there were lots of things he had to do without. He was also afraid that someone would come to his island and use force against him and he would not be able to defend himself.

In many ways, we as individuals have lots in common with Robinson Crusoe. Life would be very difficult if we did not have anyone to help us. With friends, we can feel safer, and we can share things we might not otherwise have. We can swap CDs and posters, or go to the cinema, we can play sports, and simply enjoy each other's company. If we are threatened by someone bigger and stronger than us, we may be able to call on our friends for help. Perhaps the old saying 'safety in numbers' is true!

Countries are like people. There are big countries and small countries, strong countries and weak countries. Some are rich and some are poor. Some have things like **oil** that other countries need. Countries tend to act in the same way as people.

Alliances

Countries are like people in that they look for friends that they can rely on. These friends are called **allies**, and they join together in groups called **alliances**. The countries which join in alliances agree to help each other and protect each other, just as friends do. They too, can swap **goods** with each other, just as friends do. This is called **trade**. Some countries will help their friends out in time of **need**. This is called **aid**. You may already have looked at this in the 'Rich World/Poor World' chapter.

A simple example of co-operation between countries is to ask yourself the question – Have you eaten a banana recently? If so, how can that be? We can't grow bananas in Britain.

ACTIVITY ONE

When you go home tonight, look around your home and try to make a list of at least TEN goods or products which have been bought from other countries. Try to find a variety of goods and countries, e.g. bananas from Africa, TV or video from Japan, or a car from Germany.

Reasons Why Countries Join Alliances

FRIENDSHIP

MAKING AND SELLING GOODS

TRADE
IMPORT
EXPORT

CREATE JOBS

DEFEND EACH OTHER

BRING MONEY INTO THE COUNTRY!

No country would be able to cope very well on its own, so most countries are in some kind of alliance. We are going to look at three important alliances or international organisations:

❶ the United Nations – UN;

❷ the North Atlantic Treaty Organisation – NATO;

❸ the European Union – EU.

The United Nations – the UN

A long time before you or your parents were born, the world was at war. Millions of lives were lost, and millions of pounds' worth of damage was caused. The worst ever war in history was the Second World War from 1939 to 1945. When this war ended, world leaders knew that a future war would be fought with atomic bombs, and that the destruction to life and property would be immense. The world itself might even be destroyed. They understood the importance of meeting together to discuss problems and try to prevent a Third World War. They also knew that a lot of countries who were poor and who had suffered in the past needed help. In October 1945, the 'Big Five' countries, who had been on the same side during World War Two – Britain, the USA, the USSR (now Russia), China and France – along with 46 other countries, decided to form a new international organisation to try to keep world peace. This new organisation was called the **United Nations**. The UN Building (below) is in New York, USA.

United Nations Factfile

Founded	24th October 1945
Original members	51
Members (1997)	184
Headquarters	New York
Aims	1) to keep world peace;
	2) to develop friendship between countries;
	3) to help people lead better lives;
	4) to protect individuals.
Person in charge	Secretary-General –
Previous Secretary-Generals	1) Trygve Lie – 1945–1953 – Norway
	2) Dag Hammerskjöld – 1953–1961 – Sweden
	3) U Thant – 1961–1971 – Burma
	4) Kurt Waldheim – 1971–1981 – Austria
	5) Javier Perez De Cuellar – 1981–1991 – Peru
	6) Boutros Boutros Ghali – 1991–1996 – Egypt
	7) Kofi Annan – 1996– – Ghana

❶ Why do you think the Secretary-Generals have been chosen from smaller countries?

❷ What problems might occur if the Secretary-General was from the USA or Russia?

How the United Nations is Organised

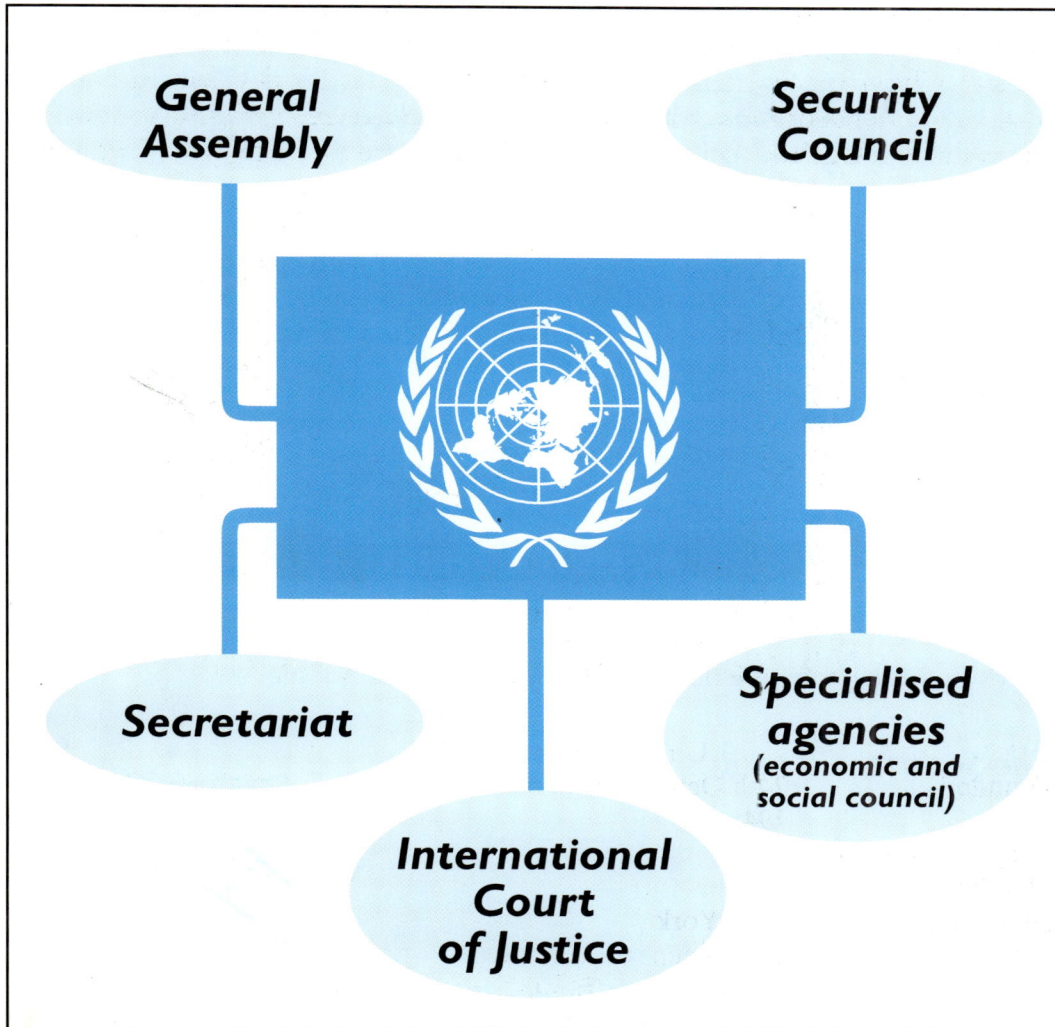

General
Assembly

Security
Council

Secretariat

Specialised
agencies
(economic and
social council)

International
Court
of Justice

The General Assembly

This is the closest thing to a World Parliament. The General Assembly is where countries meet to discuss and vote on important matters which affect the whole world. Each member country has ONE representative and ONE vote. It does not matter how big or rich or powerful a country is, it still only has ONE vote. Do you think this is fair?

Almost every country in the world is a member of the UN and takes part in the General Assembly.

By discussing important issues, the General Assembly hopes that countries will talk through their differences instead of going to war with each other. Problems that arise can be sorted out, and any future problems can be avoided. As so many countries are involved in the General Assembly, the UN has six official languages:

English   French   Spanish
Russian   Chinese   Arabic

ACTIVITY THREE

Some countries are not members of the UN. Can you find out three who are not?

Can you think of any reasons why these countries are not members?

The Security Council

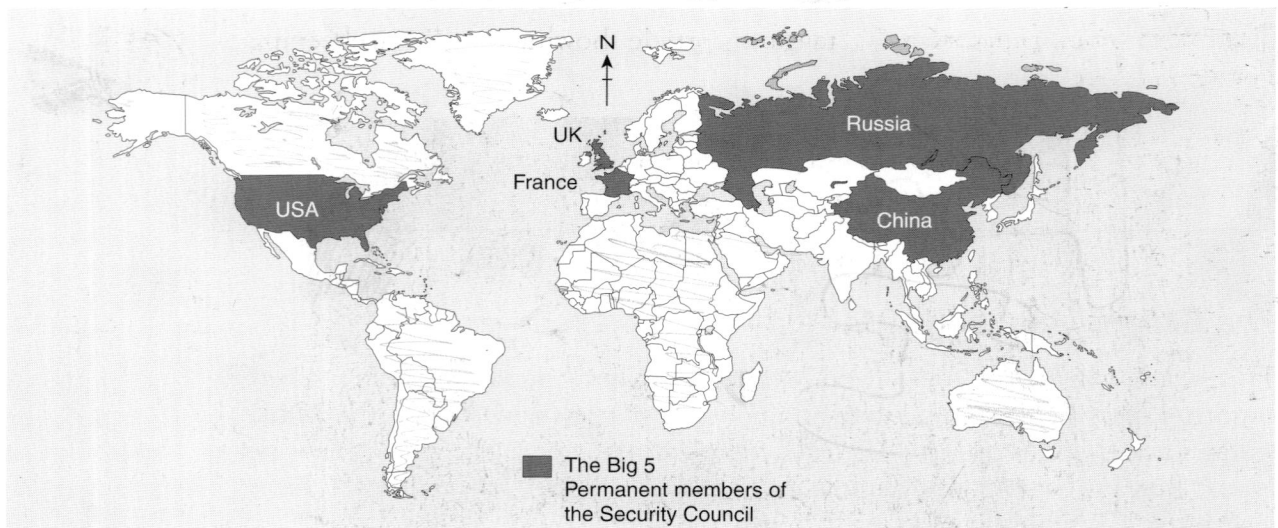

The Big 5
Permanent members of
the Security Council

The main job of the Security Council is to keep world peace and to decide whether or not to send in UN troops to try to stop fighting between member countries. The Security Council has 15 members. Five of these are **permanent members** who always have a seat on this Council and who cannot be outvoted. They are called the 'Big Five' and are Britain, the USA, Russia, China and France. The other ten are voted onto the Council by all of the members for two years, and represent countries from Asia, Africa, South America, Europe and the rest of the world. Each of the 'Big Five' has a special power called the **veto**. This means that any one of them can stop the Security Council from making a decision that they do not agree with. So, if the Security Council is to work, all of the 'Big Five' have to agree.

ACTIVITY FOUR

❶ Why do you think the 'Big Five' have this veto to stop things they don't like?

❷ Do you think it is a good idea for them to have this power of veto?

❸ What problems could arise when the security council needs to make important decisions?

UN Peacekeeping Troops

Although the UN believes in world peace, the Security Council can sometimes take the decision to send in UN troops to enforce the peace. These troops are not called an army, but are called a 'peacekeeping force'. Each member country supplies the UN with troops and equipment to make up this force. They are easily identified by their sky-blue helmets or berets, which have the UN emblem on them. You have perhaps seen them in action on the TV news. There have been many examples recently where they have been used.

ACTIVITY FIVE

Try to find a newspaper story or a magazine article showing a UN Peacekeeping Force in action.

The UN and Peacekeeping

Trying to keep world peace is perhaps the most important aim of the UN. Although there has been no major war since 1945, in every year since then there has been fighting in some part of the world. UN peacekeeping forces have been kept busy trying to stop this fighting from spreading. Sometimes they have been successful, but at other times they have not. The 1990s may have seemed fairly peaceful to us in the UK, but the UN has been very busy in various parts of the world trying to stop fighting from spreading.

The world map shows examples of UN peacekeeping troops in action in the 1990s.

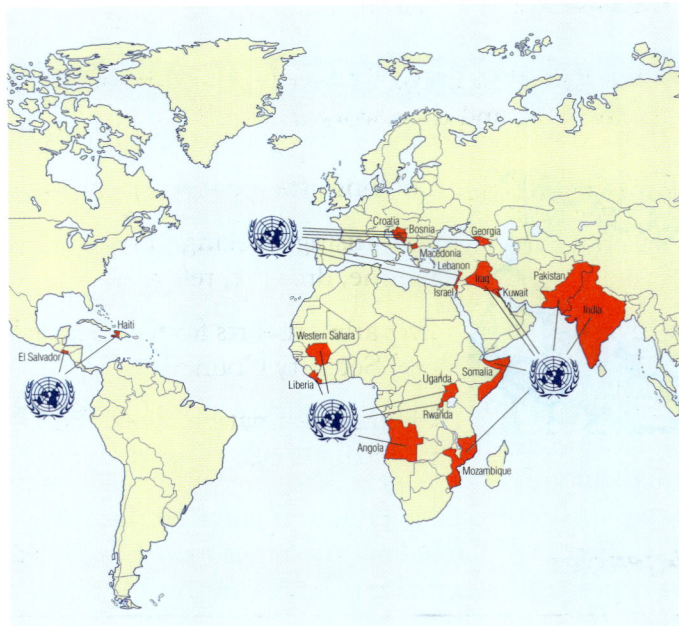

ACTIVITY SIX

❶ Watch the news on TV and add any new area to the list of countries shown on the map.

❷ Are there any other countries you know of where the UN is involved?

❸ Some people describe this part of the UN's role as that of 'world policeman'. What do you think they mean by that?

❹ Do you think this is an important part of the work of the UN? Give reasons for your answer.

The Secretariat

As the UN is such a large organisation with so many members and committees, it has a large team of full-time workers, like typists, secretaries, researchers, translators, reporters and support staff, to deal with its day-to-day running. This part of the UN is called the **Secretariat**, and is headed by the Secretary-General. Most of the people in the Secretariat are based in the UN Headquarters in New York. They are paid by the UN, which raises money through annual subscriptions from members. Each member country has to pay a membership fee to the UN, which covers expenses. Each member country will get this money from its own taxes, so we are really the ones who are paying for it.

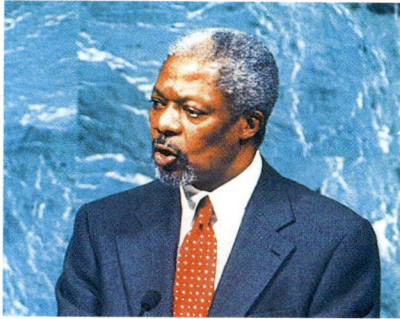

The UN Secretary General, Kofi Annan of Ghana

The Secretariat has a staff of over 16,000 people who come from almost every member country of the UN, and their work includes:

Looking after peacekeeping forces

Organising meetings on world problems like famine, drought, refugees

Preparing reports for the General Assembly and Security Council

Giving information about the UN to TV, newspapers etc.

Specialised Agencies

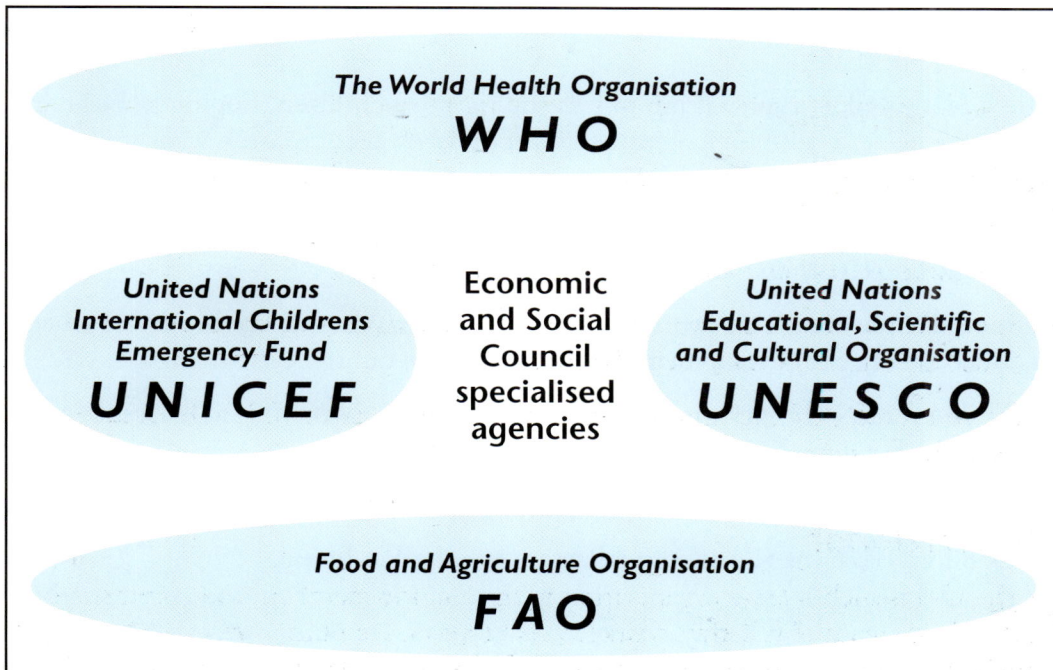

The World Health Organisation

WHO

United Nations International Childrens Emergency Fund

UNICEF

Economic and Social Council specialised agencies

United Nations Educational, Scientific and Cultural Organisation

UNESCO

Food and Agriculture Organisation

FAO

Although the main aim of the UN is to keep world peace, most of the day-to-day important work is done by the specialised agencies, which aim to improve living conditions for people in poorer countries. In the countries of the developed world, we do not see the UN doing very much, but in the developing world, the work of the specialised agencies can mean the difference between life and death for millions of people. Specialised agencies are so-called because each one has a special task to perform. There are dozens of these agencies, but FOUR of the most important ones are UNESCO, WHO, FAO and UNICEF.

ACTIVITY SEVEN

Write a few sentences explaining what you think each of the specialised agencies does to help people in the developing countries. You may have looked at these in the previous section – Rich World/Poor World, p. 77.

The International Court of Justice

This part of the UN organisation is based in The Hague in Holland and deals mainly with trying to protect human rights and freedoms. It is made up of 15 judges from different member states of the UN, who try to settle disputes between member countries.

> *All human beings are born with equal and inalienable rights and fundamental freedoms.*
>
> *In the Universal Declaration of Human Rights, the United Nations has stated in clear and simple terms the rights which belong equally to every person.*

The UN also takes a special interest in the rights of children, hoping to be able to build a better future for everyone, and to help protect children who are badly treated throughout the world.

The Convention on the Rights of the Child

Almost all countries in the world have accepted the Convention. It puts the needs of children into the development programme of all countries, including the UK.

❶ Children have the right to be with their family or those who will care for them best.

❷ Children have the right to enough food and clean water.

❸ Children have the right to an adequate standard of living.

❹ Children have the right to health care.

❺ Disabled children have the right to special care and training.

❻ Children must be allowed to speak their own language and practise their own religion and culture.

❼ Children have the right to play.

❽ Children have the right to free education.

❾ Children have the right to be kept safe and not hurt, exploited or neglected.

❿ Children must not be used as cheap labour or as soldiers.

⓫ Children have the right to rehabilitation from cruelty, neglect and injustice.

⓬ Children have the right to express their own opinions and to meet together to express their views.

(Compare these rights to the article on page 79, Rich World/Poor World, showing workers in poor countries.)

Can Anyone Join the UN?

Before a country can join the UN it must agree to TWO basic ideals:

1) to be peace-loving; 2) to obey the rules of the UN.

The rules of the UN are called the UN Charter. Here are some of its rules:

all countries have equal rights

all members agree to settle their arguments peacefully

all members will only use violence in self-defence

all members will obey the Charter

Many people think the UN is a good idea but one which does not work very well, mainly because member countries do not always agree and sometimes fail to follow the Charter. There are many examples of this, but the UN does a lot of positive work, especially in ways which do not make the headlines in the same way that wars and famines do.

Perhaps it is not good enough for people simply to say 'the UN doesn't work'. Perhaps it is up to all of us to make it work. When a previous Secretary-General of the UN was asked by a reporter, 'Does the UN work?', he replied 'Does a spade work?' Do you understand what he meant?

ACTIVITY EIGHT

Here are 15 statements about the UN. Five of them are FACTS and are correct. Five of them are examples of EXAGGERATION. Five of them are examples of BIAS. Copy and complete the table below by placing each statement in the correct column.

Fact	Exaggeration	Bias
1	1	1
2	2	2
3	3	3
4	4	4
5	5	5

Statements:

❶ Every country in the world is a member.

❷ It was set up in 1945.

❸ It now has 184 members.

❹ The UN is a waste of money.

❺ The UK should pull out of the UN.

❻ UN Day is celebrated on 24 October.

❼ The UN peacekeeping force is very powerful.

❽ There have been ten Secretary-Generals.

❾ The UN does more harm than good.

❿ The USA controls the whole of the UN.

⓫ The UK is a member of the Security Council.

⓬ The UK is the biggest country in the UN.

⓭ The UN has prevented all fighting since 1945.

⓮ The UN is successful in everything it does.

⓯ The main aim of the UN is to keep world peace.

North Atlantic Treaty Organisation (NATO)

At the end of the Second World War in 1945, the countries who formed the UN, including the Big Five, were hoping to avoid another terrible war in the future. They were not completely convinced that the UN would be strong enough to keep world peace and to protect its members from attack by other countries. Some countries felt they had to have better protection, and they decided to form a **military alliance**. This alliance meant that if any of the countries were attacked by another country, all the other countries in the alliance would help to defend it. This was known as **collective security**, which was another way of saying 'safety in numbers'.

In 1949 the countries of Western Europe, including Britain, formed a military alliance called the **North Atlantic Treaty Organisation (NATO)**. They were afraid that the Soviet Union (now Russia and other countries) was trying to take over Europe and might attack them. The Soviet Union had already taken over a number of countries in Eastern Europe at the end of the Second World War. The countries which formed NATO were:

Belgium		Italy	
Canada		Luxembourg	
Denmark		Norway	
France		Portugal	
Holland		United Kingdom	
Iceland		United States	

A few years later in the 1950s they were joined by:

West Germany (now Germany)	
Greece	
Turkey	

and in the 1980s by:

| Spain | |

The Warsaw Pact

The Soviet Union (now Russia) had its own military alliance with the countries of Eastern Europe to defend itself from an attack by NATO. This was called the **Warsaw Pact**, and its members were:

Soviet Union		Bulgaria	
East Germany (now Germany)		Romania	
Poland		Hungary	
Czechoslovakia			

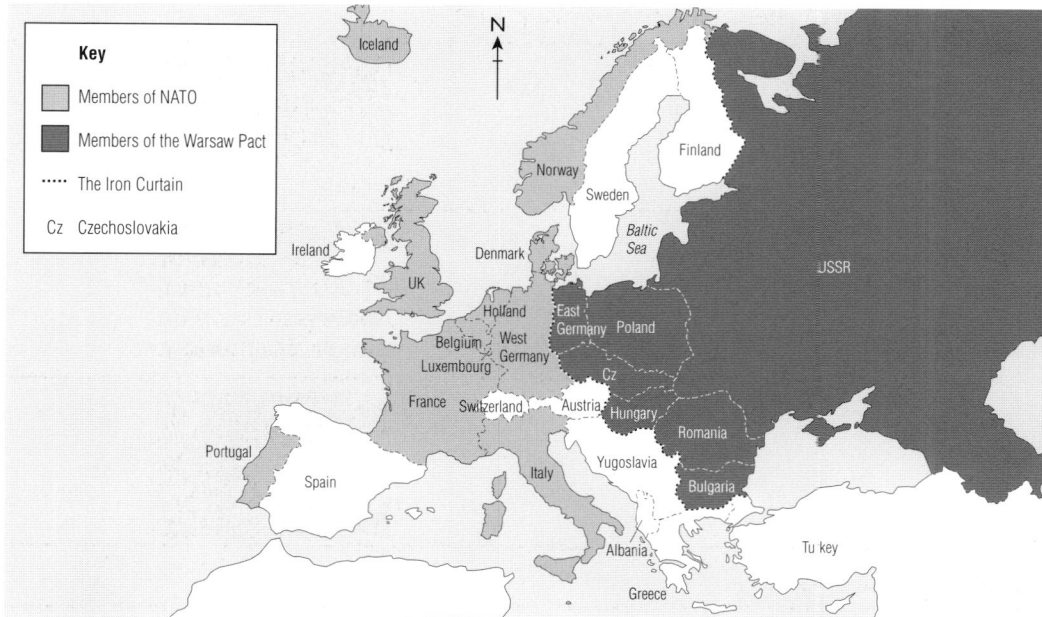

Europe, 1949

Key

Members of NATO

Members of the Warsaw Pact

..... The Iron Curtain

Cz Czechoslovakia

Iceland

N

Finland

Norway

Sweden

Baltic Sea

USSR

Denmark

Ireland

UK

Holland

East Germany Poland

Belgium West Germany

Luxembourg

Cz

France Switzerland Austria Hungary

Romania

Portugal

Spain

Italy

Yugoslavia

Bulgaria

Albania

Turkey

Greece

The Warsaw Pact no longer exists, and the countries in it are no longer under the control of the Soviet Union. Even the Soviet Union itself has been broken up into 15 different countries, with Russia being the largest. The map below shows these new states.

Former Soviet Union, 1997

ESTONIA

LATVIA

LITHUANIA

BELARUS

UKRAINE

RUSSIA

KAZAKHSTAN

MOLDAVA

GEORGIA

UZBEKISTAN

ARMENIA

TURKMENISTAN

KIRGIZSTAN

TAJIKISTAN

AZERBAIJAN

East Germany joined together again with West Germany to become Germany in 1992, and Czechoslovakia split into two states, the Czech Republic and Slovakia. Compare the map of Europe in 1949 (at the top of this page) with the map of Europe today (overleaf) and you will see many differences.

Europe, 1997

KEY
A   Albania
Ar   Armenia
Az   Azerbaijan
Be   Belgium
Cz   Czechoslovakia
De   Denmark
Es   Estonia
Sw   Switzerland
L   Luxembourg
La   Latvia
Lich Lichtenstein
Lith Lithuania
M   Moldova
Ma   Macedonia
Mo   Montenegro
Ne   Netherlands
S   Slovenia

The reason for all of this change in Eastern Europe was the collapse of Communism and the election of new democratic governments.

The Cold War

Europe from the 1950s to the 1980s was split into TWO groups of countries, each armed with very powerful nuclear weapons, and each capable of destroying the other.

NATO (led by the USA)		Warsaw Pact (led by Soviet Union)
Missile		Missile
Tank		Tank
Soldier		Soldier

One side was equally afraid of the other, and for a while Europe seemed likely to go to war again. Fortunately this did not happen, and although it was not a particularly safe time for people in Europe, the countries of NATO and the Warsaw Pact did not actually fight each other. This period became known as the **Cold War**. It did not officially end until 1991 when the Warsaw Pact was scrapped. During the Cold War, each side employed secret agents to spy on the other. The two sides tried to outdo each other in things like having the first man in space, the first Moon landing, building bigger and more powerful nuclear weapons, trying to win more friends in Africa, Asia and South America, and trying to win more gold medals than each other in the Olympics. Millions of pounds was spent developing weapons during the Cold War.

ACTIVITY NINE

❶ Compare the maps of Europe in 1949 and 1997 and list the differences.

❷ Write in your own words what you think the Cold War was.

❸ Why do you think NATO and the Warsaw Pact never actually fought?

❹ Make a list of the advantages and disadvantages of Britain being in NATO.

Do We Need NATO Now?

Many people think that since the break-up of the Soviet Union, the scrapping of the Warsaw Pact and the ending of the Cold War, Europe is a much safer place and there is no longer any need for NATO, or for Britain to be a member of this military alliance. They argue that NATO was formed to protect Europe from the old Communist Soviet Union, and now that this threat has gone, NATO is no longer needed. They argue that the millions of pounds spent on defence should now be used for more peaceful purposes like building schools and hospitals, creating more jobs, and increasing wages and pensions. This money that could be saved from defence is called the **peace dividend**. Others say NATO is still needed, as there are other countries and other leaders who remain a threat to peace in Europe and in other parts of the world.

The Future for NATO

NATO leaders themselves realise that Europe has changed and that the role of NATO will have to change also. They agreed, for example, to spend around one-third less on weapons, and to try to work better with the countries of Eastern Europe who used to be members of the Warsaw Pact. Others think NATO and the UN should move closer together, and that NATO troops and weapons could be used to strengthen the UN's peacekeeping force. If this were to happen, NATO would need to become larger and take in countries from the rest of the world. Other suggestions include training troops to help in major world disasters like earthquakes, floods and famine, and in assisting the work of the UN specialised agencies in the developing world.

Do you think we need NATO now?

How might NATO be able to change to meet the needs of its countries today?

The European Union (EU)

So far in this section on international relations, we have looked at the UN and NATO. The European Union (or EU) will help us complete the picture of three different types of international organisation.

a peacekeeping organisation

a military organisation

an economic organisation

The European Union (EU) was set up to help the countries of Europe improve their living standards, to help create jobs, to allow them to trade freely with each other, and to help rebuild much of what was destroyed in Europe by the fighting in the Second World War.

It was created in 1958, by six countries who signed the Treaty of Rome:

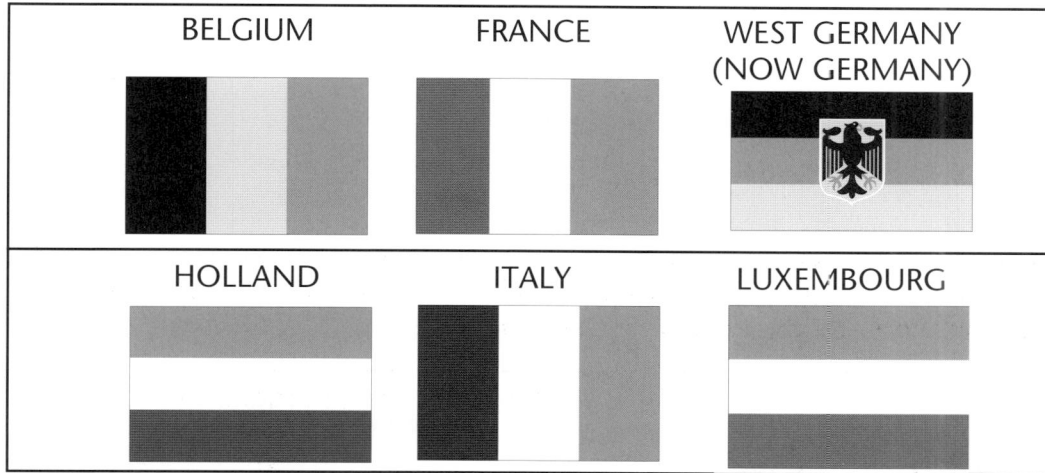

BELGIUM	FRANCE	WEST GERMANY (NOW GERMANY)

HOLLAND	ITALY	LUXEMBOURG

In 1973, three other countries joined:

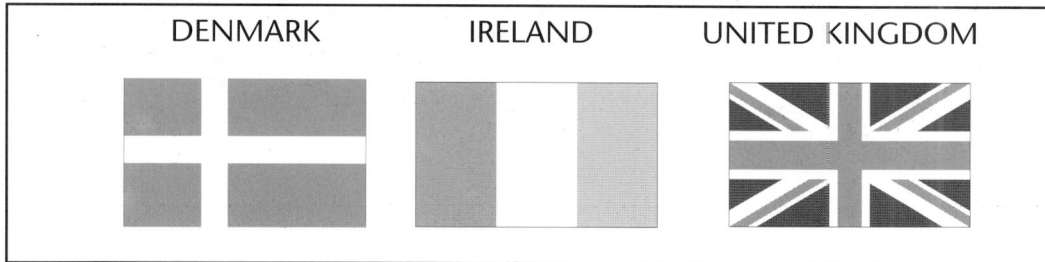

DENMARK	IRELAND	UNITED KINGDOM

In 1981, one more joined:

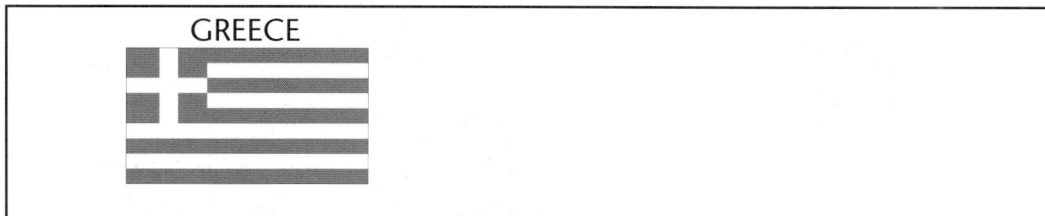

GREECE

In 1986, a further two were added:

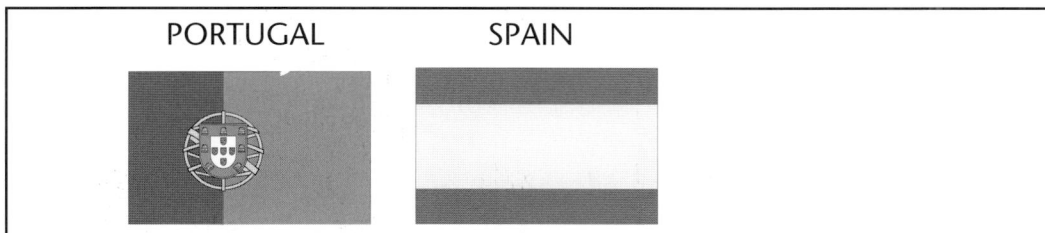

PORTUGAL	SPAIN

In 1995, three more members were admitted, making a total of 15 countries:

AUSTRIA	FINLAND	SWEDEN

Membership

The total population of the 15 member states is over 350,000,000 people, making it larger than the population of the USA, and more countries are applying to join.

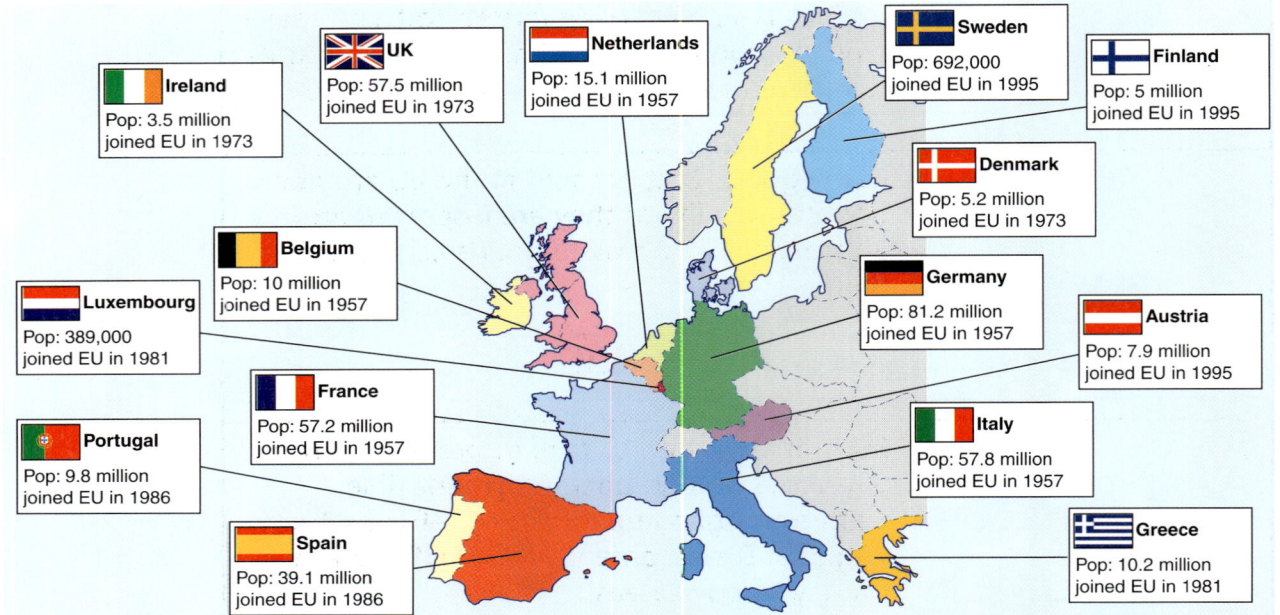

Ireland
Pop: 3.5 million
joined EU in 1973

UK
Pop: 57.5 million
joined EU in 1973

Netherlands
Pop: 15.1 million
joined EU in 1957

Sweden
Pop: 692,000
joined EU in 1995

Finland
Pop: 5 million
joined EU in 1995

Belgium
Pop: 10 million
joined EU in 1957

Denmark
Pop: 5.2 million
joined EU in 1973

Luxembourg
Pop: 389,000
joined EU in 1981

Germany
Pop: 81.2 million
joined EU in 1957

Austria
Pop: 7.9 million
joined EU in 1995

France
Pop: 57.2 million
joined EU in 1957

Italy
Pop: 57.8 million
joined EU in 1957

Portugal
Pop: 9.8 million
joined EU in 1986

Spain
Pop: 39.1 million
joined EU in 1986

Greece
Pop: 10.2 million
joined EU in 1981

The European Union has had various names during its lifetime. When it was set up in 1958, it was called the **European Economic Community** (EEC). In the 1980s this was shortened to the **European Community** (EC). It is now more properly called the **European Union** (EU).

ACTIVITY ELEVEN

❶ List the 15 member states of the European Union in order of population, starting with the largest.

❷ What other names has the European Union been called in the past?

❸ When did the United Kingdom become a member?

Why do Countries Become Members of the EU?

	Members can trade with each other without having to pay duties and taxes. This helps to keep the cost of goods down.
	Europe is now a powerful trading group and can compete with economically strong countries like the USA. The countries of Europe could not do this individually.

	People from the member states, and this includes you, can go to live and work in any other country in the EU, without any restrictions.
	Various laws have been passed to try to make working conditions in all of the member states safer and to improve wages in each country.
	Many goods that are sold in the EU are now of better quality as they are inspected and approved. EU approved goods carry a special mark. CE
	EU money is used to help improve farming and areas of high unemployment. The Common Agricultural Policy (CAP) and the Regional Development Fund (RDF) both give money to poor areas.
	The EU Social Fund can give grants and help to improve things like education, sport and leisure activities, and also to help people find jobs.
	A special fund can help countries improve their tourism, and assist individual people to set up their own businesses.
	The EU also helps to develop friendship among the member countries.

How Much does All This Cost?

Like every big organisation, the EU costs a great deal of money to run, and each member state has to pay a certain amount each year towards the costs. The wealthier countries have to pay more than the poorer countries – just like the UN!

Not all countries receive the same benefits from membership. Some countries, and some parts of countries known as regions, get a lot more money from the EU than they pay in. This is because they are poorer and receive more help.

ACTIVITY TWELVE

❶ Do you think it is fair that not all member countries of the EU pay the same amount or receive the same amount each year?

❷ Using different sources, like the school library, CD ROM, Internet, reference books, EU publications, etc, try to find out how much each member country of the EU pays each year in annual contributions, and make a bar graph of this. Then try to find out how much each member country of the EU receives in the same year. Make a second bar graph. When you have completed the graphs, compare the information and make two lists – one headed A+ for the countries who receive more than they pay in, and one headed A– for countries who pay in more than they receive. Do the results surprise you?

The EU has helped lots of different parts of Scotland to do things like:

build new roads
open new leisure complexes and swimming pools
build new rail links and stations
give help to Scottish farmers
build new industrial estates – Enterprise Zones
give help to Scottish fishermen

Look around your area and see whether you can find anything that has been done with EU help – there might be signs nearby showing the EU logo.

European Money

One of the aims of the EU is to introduce a single European Currency Unit (ECU) which would replace all types of money being used in the different countries. Everyone in the EU would then use the same money and there would be no need to exchange money into foreign currency when you travel from one EU country to another. The 15 member states and their currencies are all mixed up below. Can you match them?

Austria	Franc
Belgium	Schilling
Finland	Krone
France	Franc
Germany	Guilder
Greece	Drachma
Holland	Lira
Italy	Punt

Denmark	Escudo
Luxembourg	Peseta
Ireland	Pound
Portugal	Markka
Spain	Franc
United Kingdom	Krona
Sweden	Mark

EU Currency

Here are some samples of recent suggestions from the EU of how the new currency might look:

(Source: *Europe at a Glance* EU Publication)

(Source: *Europe Today* EU Publication)

There will be seven Euro notes: 5, 10, 20, 50, 100, 200 and 500 ECUs. Each will be a different size and colour. There will be eight coins: 1, 2, 5, 10, 20 and 50 cents and 1 and 2 ECUs. The EU hopes to have these in use by January 2002.

Should Britain Stay in the EU?

Not everyone is happy with this idea of Britain being a member of the EU. Some politicians think the EU has grown too big and costs the UK too much money.

Some people think the EU makes too many laws which British people do not like or think are not good for us. They argue that Parliament in London should make the laws for the UK, and that the EU should not be able to change or overrule these laws. The politicians who think this way are sometimes called **Eurosceptics**.

How is the EU Organised?

Like other big organisations such as the UN or NATO, the EU is divided up into different parts, each responsible for running a different section of the organisation. The most important parts of the EU are:

The Council of Ministers

The European Parliament

The Commission

The European Court

The Council of Ministers

It is here that the really important decisions of the EU are made. Each member country sends ONE of its Government Ministers to the Council. This is perhaps like the General Assembly of the UN except that not every country has ONE vote. The bigger members have more votes than the smaller ones.

Germany, France, Italy and the United Kingdom:	10 votes
Spain:	8 votes
Belgium, Greece, the Netherlands and Portugal:	5 votes
Austria and Sweden:	4 votes
Ireland, Denmark and Finland:	3 votes
Luxembourg:	2 votes
Total	87 votes

The European Commission

The European Commission meets in Brussels. It can be compared to the Secretariat of the UN, as it deals with the day-to-day running of the EU. It has a very large office staff to help put the decisions of the Council of Ministers into practice.

The European Parliament

This part of the EU meets in Strasbourg in France.

Each member state elects a number of European MPs (MEPs) to send to the European Parliament. MEPs are elected for five years. The last Euro-elections were in June 1994, which means that the next elections will be in June 1999. The country is divided up into large areas for the European elections.

The number of MEPs each country has depends on its population. The larger the country in population terms, the more MEPs it has.

Table of number of Euro MPs for each member state

> **Members:** 626 elected every 5 years: Germany 99, France, Italy, the United Kingdom 87 each, Spain 64, the Netherlands 31, Belgium, Greece and Portugal 25 each, Sweden 22, Austria 21, Denmark and Finland 16 each, Ireland 15, Luxembourg 6. Next election due 1999.

The European Parliament is not a very good name for this part of the EU, as this parliament does not make laws like many other parliaments. It is the Council of Ministers which makes the most important decisions. The European Parliament can make suggestions to the Council and try to persuade it to change certain laws.

Glenys Kinnock is the Euro MP for South Wales East.

The European Court

This part of the EU meets in Luxembourg. The Court has judges and can be compared to the International Court of Justice. It can decide and settle arguments between member countries, but perhaps more importantly, individual people can take their cases to the European Court if they think they have been treated unfairly by the courts in their own country. It was the European Court which caused the banning of corporal punishment in Scottish schools. Ask your parents and grandparents whether they remember getting 'the belt' at school!

The European Union – is it worth it?

Let's look at an average day of a family . . .

You get up and take a bath and boil the kettle – EU water quality standards ensure that water is safe for human consumption. You put some bread in the toaster – EU regulations ensure that all electrical appliances are safe and encourage them to be energy-efficient. Whether you have marmalade or a bowl of muesli – EU rules ensure that all foodstuffs are labelled properly, giving clear indications of price, sell-by dates and a list of ingredients and additives. If children around the house play with their toys – EU rules make sure that toys pass safety standards;

In the street you may well grumble about car exhaust fumes – the EU has taken the lead in tightening emission standards for cars, lorries and other means of transport;

At school, of course, you or your children will learn foreign languages – this can lead to job opportunities abroad in the future;

In your area you might notice the construction of a new bridge, a new motorway, a new business centre – EU money is given to infrastructure projects which help regions suffering from industrial decline, rural depopulation and high unemployment;

The company you or your parents work for might see the benefits of exporting its goods – this is now much easier and can be quite profitable. It is important to know that 'health and safety' rules protect workers in the workplace, for example from excessive noise or exposure to dangerous substances. EU rules ensure good conditions of employment – for example a woman must be paid the same as a man would for doing the same job. New mothers can also enjoy adequate maternity leave.

(Source: *Europe Today*, EU Publication.)

ACTIVITY THIRTEEN

❶ Class discussion – ask your teacher to divide the class into TWO groups, one in favour of the EU and one against it. The question is whether or not Britain should stay in the EU. Try to find sensible arguments to support your group's point of view.

❷ You should also try to find out the address of the EU and get the class to write a letter to them asking for information about the EU. You will get lots of material back. The article above from *Europe Today* is a sample of some material published for schools by the EU. In what ways might someone who does not support the EU say this information is biased?

❸ Find out the name of your MEP. Write a letter explaining that you are studying the EU as part of your 5–14 Environmental Studies 'People in Society' course and invite them to your school to talk about their job.

123

European Timeline

The following diagram shows you some of the main events in Europe since the Second World War: copy and keep the timeline up to date by adding important events as they happen.

1945	1949	1952	1955
End of WW2 UN set up	NATO formed	Greece and Turke join NATO	West Germany joins NATO
			1955
			Soviet Union forms Warsaw Pact

1981	1973	1960s	1958
Greece joins EEC	UK, Ireland and Denmark join EEC	Cold War begins	EEC set up by six countries
1982			
Spain joins NATO			

1986	1989	1990	1991
Spain and Portugal join EEC	Berlin Wall comes down	End of Cold War	Warsaw Pact ends
			1991
			Communism ends in the Soviet Union

1995	1992	1992	1992
Austria Sweden, Finland join EU	Yugoslavia splits; Czechoslovakia too	East and West Germany re-unite	Soviet Union splits into 15 new states
1998			

1999	2000	2001	2002